THE ROMAN
CONQUEST
OF BRITAIN

1 *The Emperor Claudius*

From a bust, first century A.D.

THE ROMAN CONQUEST OF BRITAIN

A.D 43-57

DONALD R. DUDLEY & GRAHAM WEBSTER

DUFOUR EDITIONS 1965

First published 1965

Library of Congress Catalog Card Number: 65-26317

MADE AND PRINTED IN GREAT BRITAIN FOR
DUFOUR EDITIONS, INC.
CHESTER SPRINGS, PENNSYLVANIA 19425

PREFACE

It was with some misgiving that we accepted the publisher's invitation to contribute to the series on British Battles a book about the Claudian Invasion of Britain. The battles with which we shall have to deal are neither uninteresting nor unimportant; after all, they determined the history of this island for more than three centuries. But the evidence at our command is of an altogether different nature from that available to the modern military historian. He has official dispatches, the reports of war-correspondents, maps, battle-plans, films, photographs, and private accounts and diaries in almost embarrassing profusion and detail. For example, in the account of the Alma, in a companion volume, we read that 'his [Sir George Brown's] contribution to the battle had so far been nil, but he was reputed to have been the only man in the army to have shaved that morning'. Again: 'only when this had been done to the satisfaction of Colonel Mauleverer of the 30th did he resume his place in the line and was heard unconcernedly asking Major Patullo for a light for his cigar'. Such particularity is not for the historian of the Claudian Invasion.

But our problems go deeper. We have two major battles, neither of which can be placed on the map with absolute confidence. The lines of the Roman advance to the Severn, the Humber, and the Exe are known only in the most general way, even if their terminal points are fairly certain. At a later phase, forts and military roads impose a more reliable geographical pattern; we are better informed of the way in which the Romans consolidated their conquests in Britain than that by which they were won. As all who have tried it know too well, there is a fundamental difficulty about trying to combine the two kinds of evidence we have—that of the scanty historical texts and that of archaeology. The two sort ill together: the narrative of battles should move fast, the evidence of archaeology must be

7

presented in detailed and sometimes tedious argument. Some of this we have tried to reserve for the Appendices and Notes, hoping thus to provide a fairly unencumbered text for those whose interest is rather in military history than in Roman Britain. Even so, we fear this book will be an awkward recruit when it comes to stand in line with Balaclava and Malplaquet, with Waterloo and El Alamein.

We have to acknowledge help and advice from many sources, and notably from Lady Aileen Fox, Professor Eric Birley, Mr Leo Rivet, Dr Michael Jarrett, Mr R. F. Jessup, and Mr Arnold Baker. Professor Harry Thorpe, Dr John Wilkes and Mr Anthony Birley, our colleagues in Birmingham, have given us the benefit of expert knowledge on several points. Our thanks are also due to Mr Frederick Reed for reading the text and indicating ambiguities, and to Mrs Muriel Stanley for undertaking the arduous task of compiling the index. If we have still contrived to make mistakes, they are entirely our own.

Birmingham, 1964   D.R.D.

G.W.

CONTENTS

THE ILLUSTRATIONS

ACKNOWLEDGMENT

The authors and publishers wish to thank the following for the illustrations appearing in this book:

Aerofilms and Aero Pictorial Ltd for figs 12 and 16; Musée Calvet, Avignon for fig. 6; Arnold Baker for figs 35, 37, 38 and 40; Bridport and Bristol Museums for fig. 27; the Trustees of the British Museum for figs 13, 25 and 29; Chichester Photographic Service Ltd for fig. 43; Corinium Museum, Cirencester for fig. 26; Colchester and Essex Museum for figs 2 and 4; M. B. Cookson for figs 17 and 20–22; Dorset County Museum for fig. 28; Professor S. S. Frere and Dr Edward Johnson for fig. 32; The Society for the Promotion of Roman Studies and Lincoln Archaeological Research Committee for fig. 30; Altertumsmuseum, Mainz for fig. 3; Mansell Collection for fig. 1; Newark Museum for fig. 31; Dr J. K. St Joseph for fig. 33; Helga Schmidt-Glassner for fig. 8; Society of Antiquaries of London for figs 10, 17 and 20–22; Kunsthistorisches Museum, Vienna for fig. 14; The National Museum of Wales for figs 7 and 41; Dr Graham Webster for figs 5 and 44; the West Midlands Photographic Services Ltd for figs 45–47; Sir Mortimer Wheeler for figs 17 and 20–22.

NOTE

The italicised numerals in the text, placed in parentheses, refer to the figure numbers of the illustrations.

Roman
Preparations

I

Early in the spring of A.D. 43, the coast of Gaul opposite the chalk cliffs of Britain was the scene of great activity. A vast array of troops and horses had been gradually assembling since the end of winter. From all the small harbours along the coast ships were being sailed or towed to the port of embarkation. In the shipyards swarms of workmen were busy repairing and building new craft. Along the new roads to the Channel ports trundled the waggons loaded with stores and equipment from every part of Gaul. Plans were well advanced for the Great Invasion. The Emperor Claudius, two years on the throne and in his early fifties, saw an opportunity for gaining a triumph in Britain which would round off the distinguished achievements of his kinsmen, Drusus and Germanicus, and of himself, in the north-western provinces.

Much care had been taken in selecting the high command and staff, as was usual in the reign of Claudius. The commander-in-chief was Aulus Plautius, who was connected with the Emperor through his kinswoman Plautia Urgulanilla, Claudius' first wife. One of the most distinguished senators of the day, Plautius had held the consulship in A.D. 29, and was Governor of Pannonia at the time of his appointment to the British expedition. There he will have had experience of a warlike frontier, though we can give no details of his military career. His task must have been to supervise the assembly of the expeditionary force, conduct it across the Channel, and command at least the first phases of military operations, depending on the degree of British resistance encountered. He would then become Governor of Britain, and organise that part of it selected for development as a Roman province. Among the legionary commanders was the future Emperor Vespasian, then in charge of the IInd *Augusta* and with his service honours to come, and accompanied by his older brother Flavius Sabinus, and also Hosidius Geta, who had so recently distinguished himself in Mauretania.[1] The size and composition of the expeditionary force had been carefully considered, bearing in mind the lessons learned from the campaigns of Julius Caesar. Caesar had taken two legions and an unstated number of cavalry on his first invasion in 55 B.C.; five legions 'and an equal force of cavalry' on the second in 54 B.C.[2] Careful attention had been given to the cavalry force for the Claudian expedition and an unusual command, that of *praefectus equitatus,* assigned to Didius Gallus, the third governor of Britain (A.D. 52–58?).[3] Four legions were assigned for the operations of Aulus Plautius, perhaps with detachments from others, including probably the VIIIth Legion and the number of auxiliaries will have brought the force up to 40–50,000 men.

The Rhine command had allocated three legions for the invasion, the IInd *Augusta* from Argentoratum (Strasbourg), the XXth *Valeria* from Novaesium (Neuss), the XIV *Gemina* from Moguntiacum (Mainz). The remaining legion of the force came from the Danube command, probably from Siscia (Sisak) in Pannonia.[4] This was the IXth *Hispana,* and it probably made the long journey of more than a thousand miles as escort to the commander-in-chief. All were legions with experience of warfare in Northern Europe. The IInd, raised by Augustus, had served in Spain, but was moved to Germany in A.D. 10. The IXth had also been in Spain, before its transfer to the Danube some time earlier than A.D. 6. The XIVth, another Augustan legion, which was to distinguish itself in Britain, had served in Illyricum and Germany. The XXth had served under Tiberius in the Pannonian rebellion, after which it was sent to the Rhine. The auxiliary units included men from Gaul, Thrace and Germany: the presence of Batavian troops who were experts in river-crossings is especially notable.[5]

So far, the Roman staff-work had been of a high order. But battles are won, in part, in soldiers' minds, and for this great enterprise the psychological preparation had been less than thorough. This showed itself when, preparations complete, the order was given to embark. Suddenly the commanders discovered the baleful influence of the Ocean, and the almost pathological dread it aroused in the invasion force. This sprang from many causes. To the geographers of the Greek and Roman world Britain was a monstrous aberration—quite literally, it ought not to be there. It could be shown by reason that the habitable world was bounded on all sides by the Ocean, and that no lands or islands lay beyond. Except for the British Isles, and they—against all the rules—contained the largest island known to Roman science![6] It was wrong; Britain, although (regrettably) it existed, must form 'another world' (*alter orbis*). So the geographers. But, to the superstitious soldiers, Britain was a land of mystery. Travellers' tales went round the camps, and lost nothing in the telling. The legions from Germany had grim experience of the hazards of warfare in northern waters. Few passages of Tacitus are more dramatic than the account of the great surge of the North Sea that trapped and wrecked the expeditionary force of Germanicus between the mouths of the Ems and the Rhine in the autumn of A.D. 16.[7] A few survivors of the storm-battered Roman Fleet were swept across to Britain and later returned by the island chiefs. 'Not a man', says Tacitus, 'returned from a distance without his story of marvels—terrible hurricanes, unknown birds, sea-monsters, creatures half-human and half-bestial—all of which they had seen, or believed in their fear.' More soberly, the historian adds his own comment '. . . that Ocean is more stormy than any of the other seas of the world'. For a Roman force to cross the Channel and invade Britain meant the shattering of barriers that were as much psychological as physical. They had been too strong for the force assembled by the megalomaniac Emperor Gaius, three or four years earlier, though what truth lies behind the strange tale recorded by the historians on that occasion we do not know. Certainly Gaius was forced to call off the invasion, the only achievement of which was the building of a lighthouse at Boulogne.

And now the troops of Claudius, agog with wild rumour and knowing that the previous expedition had never sailed, refused to embark.[8] It was a critical moment for the military commander. The troops could hardly be treated with the harsh discipline usual for desertion or cowardice in the face of the enemy. A bold and imaginative commander might have won them over by his force of personality, but Aulus Plautius was not such a man. He was at a disadvantage in that three of his four legions were from the Rhine command, and he had had little time to enforce his authority over them. Perhaps, too, he did not understand how deep-seated was their dread of the unknown island. So he played for safety, and spread his responsibility by appealing for guidance from the Emperor. A confidential agent was sent in the person of Narcissus, an Imperial freedman, and the story goes that the soldiers were at first enraged that a man who had previously been a slave should deign to address them, mounted on the tribunal of the commander-in-chief. But the comic irony of the situation struck them and their contempt turned to derision and to shouts of '*io Saturnalia*'; for at the Saturnalia the slaves wore their masters' costumes and gave the orders. The real state of affairs in the administration of Claudius had not penetrated to the army camps along the Rhine. For the freedmen did give the orders, and Narcissus may well have played a part in the planning of the British expedition. Having thus worked off their bad humour, the troops quietly embarked. These are obviously the very bare bones of a strange story. Narcissus must have been a highly intelligent and able man to have been selected for the post he held, equivalent to a Permanent Secretary. No doubt a clever Greek might use subtle methods on the Romans with their stolid outlook. His oration, with its calculated broad humour, may have been the final stage in a complex process of restoring morale and removing doubts and difficulties provoked by the invasion.

But the result of the near-mutiny was a serious delay, and Dio Cassius says it made the Roman departure late in the season.[9] Although it is not specifically stated, it would seem from this that Narcissus was sent by Claudius from Rome. An Imperial courier service had been established by Augustus and staging-posts were available along all the main roads, maintained by the local authorities through whose district they passed. Some very fast times are on record for emergencies, but the couriers used four-wheeled enclosed carts and achieved an average speed of about five miles an hour. On special occasions relays of gallopers could maintain an average of ten miles an hour day and night.[10] It is thus hardly likely that the messenger sent by Plautius would have taken less than five days to reach Massilia, where he would have embarked for Rome, adding another three to six days on the voyage. Narcissus, on the other hand, an important state official, would not have proceeded at this rate, but with a large train of attendants would have taken two or three times as long. From the time Plautius dispatched his messenger to the arrival of Narcissus may have been up to two months, and it was probably well into July before the fleet sailed.

II

Before we follow the armada across the Channel, digressions must be made to consider in brief, first, the organisation and equipment of the Roman Army and its opponents, and, secondly, the lessons that had been learned on both sides from the invasions of Julius Caesar.

The Praetorians, or Imperial Bodyguard, a *corps d'élite*, only took the field when led by the Emperor in person. They were normally based on Rome. The legions formed the backbone of the army, and there were then twenty-seven of these formations. They were tough, well-trained, disciplined infantry, made up of Roman citizens. Recruitment in the west was limited at this time to Italy, Spain and Gaul and the Roman *coloniae*. There were still in the legions many men from Italy itself, although gradually the extension of the franchise and foundation of *coloniae* introduced more and more men from the outer regions of the Roman world. A legion was composed of ten cohorts, each of 480 men, except the first, which was double that number. The cohorts consisted of six centuries of eighty men. Attached to the legion was a small body of horsemen whose main duties were those of dispatch riders and guards; they could not be regarded as an effective cavalry force. At this period the emphasis was on the foot soldier who bore the brunt of the fighting; the use of cavalry as shock troops came only later. There were also many specialists—clerks for stores and records, armourers and black-smiths, master stone-masons and carpenters, artificers of all kinds, and of course medical staff. The legion had its own architect and water engineer but these, like doctors and surgeons, were regarded merely as technicians.

The legionaries were uniformly equipped with body armour which at this time may have been undergoing a change. The jerkin of hardened leather reinforced with metal plates was being replaced by the more complicated strip armour (*lorica segmentata*). This is seen in its fully developed form on Trajan's Column (*36*). There are back and front plates giving protection up to the neck, and over these are the curved overlapping steel strips, hinged at the back and fastened with thongs laced into hooks at the front. To give flexibility of movement the strips had to slide one over the other, for had they been fastened separately to the jerkin below they would have had the effect of a steel corset. In the scenes from the Column, the armoured soldiers are shown in many postures, engaged in strenuous activities which demand complete freedom. This armour only came as far as the hips: below this the only protection was from the apron made of leather and bronze strips hanging from the belt, which swung sporran-like between the legs without interfering with movement. The helmet was a well-designed piece of equipment: like the lorica it was going through a phase of development at this period. The older type was like a jockey cap with bronze dome and a horizontal projection at the back; only the brow-ridge gave protection at the front, apart from the pair of hinged cheek-pieces. This simple robust bronze helmet was being replaced by a composite form with an iron skull cap, the main difference being the deeper protection at the back of the neck, where lay the great weakness of the other type. The legionary shield was of a large semi-cylindrical type, which when held close to the body gave protection from the chin to the thigh along the whole of one side. In spite of its size it was probably fairly light, being made of a kind of plywood; it was bound only at the edges in metal and had a strong bronze central boss for the internal hand-grip. The outer surface was covered with red leather, on which there were gilded bronze patterns representing the thunderbolts of Jupiter. On the march, the soldiers carried their shields by a strap over the head so that they hung down the left side: they were held only in battle conditions. The arm slid through a leather loop so that the main weight of the shield rested on the forearm rather than the hand itself.

The attacking weapons were the javelin (*pilum*) and the short sword (*gladius*). The wooden *pilum* was seven foot long with an iron shank having a hardened point. Each legionary carried two of these; they were thrown in volleys from distances of about forty and thirty

2 M. Favonius Facilis, a centurion
of the XXth Legion

From his tombstone at Colchester

3 A soldier of the XIVth 'Gemina'

From a tombstone at Mainz

(For explanation of inscriptions,
see Appendix IV, p. 189)

4 *An auxiliary cavalryman*

From the tombstone of Longinus at Colchester

(See Appendix IV, p. 189)

5 *Detail from a cavalry tombstone at Cirencester*

yards. They were not so much for killing as for disarming the enemy. The hard point pierced the enemy shield held up in defence and the shank bent under the weight of the *pilum*. It could not be easily withdrawn, so that the shield had to be discarded. The legionaries then drew their short swords and engaged the enemy in close work, with the great defensive advantage—as compared with a barbarian enemy—of having large close-fitting shields and body armour. The sword was used for stabbing, like the modern bayonet. The Celts were used to open warfare where they could swing their long swords against individual targets. The Roman legionaries were trained to fight in close formation and pressed constantly on the enemy in a tight mêlée, where the short sword could be used more effectively. The long, curved Roman shield was useful in protecting the left side when held close; in the attack it could be thrust forward to knock the enemy off balance and so provide a target for the sword. This was used with an upward jab and plenty of wrist action. The Celtic method of fighting was based on individual combat, and against their warriors the close assault of legionaries in their tight formations proved most effective. The Romans had another great advantage in the training of their units. The Celts could be heroic fighters under inspired leadership, but they had no effective organisation; once the battle was joined it was difficult to direct and manœuvre particular sections. With the Roman organisation this was no obstacle. With prearranged signals given by trumpets or bugles, centuries or cohorts could be disengaged, and the direction of attack turned as weaknesses in the enemy line were found and exploited.

While the main frontal assaults were delivered by the legionaries, another branch of the army, the *auxilia*, played their part on the flanks. As their name implies, these troops were first regarded as aids to the legions. They were recruited originally from barbarian tribes and retained their names and methods of fighting. While at first in pre-Augustan days they were sometimes an ill-organised rabble of locals liable to desert at a critical moment, they later became an integral part of the Roman Army. Augustus, with his peculiar genius, rationalised the situation by gradually turning them into a permanent force. They were levied from almost every province of the Roman

Empire except Achaea (Greece), and in special cases this levy was preferred to tribute or requisitions of other kinds. In the late Republic, citizenship had been conferred on certain units for outstanding services, but it may have been Claudius who made this important provision for all auxiliaries who completed an honourable period of service. There was thus an incentive to join this branch of the army, and its total effect over the first two centuries of Imperial rule in extending the franchise must have been very considerable. By the end of the first century A.D. there may have been as many as 200,000 auxiliaries in the army. As each served twenty-five years there would thus (allowing for casualties) have been five or six thousand new citizens every year; add to this the wives and children, and over the first two centuries, at a modest estimate, the total may well have been up to five million new citizens through this source alone. At this period all the units were of cohort strength, i.e. about five hundred men. There were basically three types of unit,[11] the cavalry *ala,* the part-mounted unit and the infantry cohort, in that order of status. The number of units raised varied with the population in each province. Thus there were (about A.D. 100) at least thirty-two cohorts of Gauls, thirteen of Britons, nine of Batavians, fifteen of Raetians, eight of Dalmatians, six of Asturians, thirty-nine from Gallia Belgica (including the two Germanies) and sixty from Spain, while there were at least eight Thracian cavalry *alae*, upwards of twenty from Gaul, one *ala* of *Dromedarii*, and so on. Each group of units so raised would have been organised in the same manner, but equipped in their native style. In this way the army had troops with a great variety of specialist experience. The infantry might be lightly armed and mobile with throwing spear, or heavily armed and static, with a heavy spear like a pike to break up a cavalry charge. There were several kinds of missile users, from archers to slingers and stone-throwers. Cavalry likewise varied in their armour and weapons. One has only to study the great variety of spears, lances and javelins found on Roman military sites to appreciate their complexity.[12]

One of the important aspects of the army from the archaeologist's point of view is that of their forts and camps, since it is from the excavation of these that much of our information is obtained. When

the army was campaigning in Gaul under Caesar in the first century
B.C., the troops were always housed in tents. There is no indication
of a permanent fort with buildings. During the winter, army groups
were settled down in a selected area in their *hiberna*, but even these
still lived in tents. In the summer campaigns the army always constructed a fortified camp for the night; the tents were set out in an
orderly array on a carefully constructed grid pattern, the unit being
organised in strict order of seniority round the central tent which
housed the commander and his staff. The streets or through-ways
were of particular importance for the rapid assembly of horses and
men at any danger point. There is an interesting passage in which
Caesar relates how he deliberately reduced the size of a fort by cutting down the width of the roads in order to deceive the Gauls as to
the size of the force. This suggests a degree of standardisation by
which the enemy could estimate with reasonable accuracy the size of
the Roman army facing them by the area of their camps. Under
normal circumstances, when an army was on the march, the defences
of most camps consisted of a ditch only about a yard wide and deep.
The bank on the inside was made of stacked turves, to which was
added the spoil from the ditch; on to the top were fixed the palisade
stakes (*pila muralia*), each about seven feet long. Each man was
allocated two of these stakes, and from this it can be estimated that
they would be about six inches apart in the bank, and tied together at
the centre. The result was an adequate fence to keep stray animals
out, and soldiers with a tendency to wander, inside the camp, but
against a serious attack these defences were not very formidable. The
Roman Army was at this period an attacking force and these camps
were not intended to withstand sieges; it was much more effective to
engage the enemy in the open. There were occasions, however, when
it was necessary to dig in. This is illustrated by another episode from
Caesar when he needed to deceive the Gauls by pretending to be
afraid. The legionaries were ordered to raise the height of the ramparts and block the gateways with turves and then withdraw men
from the ramparts. The Gauls thought the gates would be the most
strongly held points, so they began to fill in the ditches and pull
down the bank beyond; while they were so engaged the Romans
slipped out of the rear gates and attacked them so unexpectedly that

the Gauls, although in some strength, were put to flight. It is clear from this that in some cases mere tented enclosures could have considerable defences. This seems to be true of Britain. The larger fort at Metchley in Birmingham has a double ditch and large rampart, but no sign of permanent buildings within. Evidence from Waddon Hill in Dorset also suggests that the defences were first erected by quarrying the hill-top, just as the Britons did for their hill-forts; only later was the interior levelled out and the quarry pits filled in for the erection of timber buildings.

In contrast to the camps, perhaps better referred to as marching camps, are the permanent forts with their timber barracks and other buildings. Here the unit has settled down in a position for an indefinite period. It was between the period of Caesar and Claudius that the idea of the permanent fort came into being. Along the Rhine and Danube frontiers the army gradually consolidated and in the hard winters the tented quarters would have been a source of grievance to the soldiers. Although this grievance was not stressed during the mutinies on the Rhine under Tiberius, it is clear that a change of policy was desirable. By the time Britain was invaded, the men could expect to be provided with permanent buildings, having timber and clay walls to keep out the wind, rain and snow. These buildings at first were laid out like tents; only by the Flavian period was their internal planning rationalised into a stereotyped text-book pattern. Much later most of the principal buildings were built of stone, and with this comes also the inscription in permanent form. Whereas from the northern garrisons there is a great mass of epigraphic material from which it is possible to learn many details of chronology and of the names of units, in the first century these inscriptions would have been carved on wood panels, and none survive.[12] Archaeological evidence for dating is thus confined to a study of coins, pottery, brooches, and similar objects which may by their changes of fashion yield such information.

The third branch of the Roman Army was the fleet.[13] There is little doubt that at this period its organisation was flexible and varied according to circumstances. Basically it was not considered as a fighting arm and thus was ranked as inferior to the *auxilia*. The main duties of the fleet were to transport troops and stores across the seas and over large rivers where a bridge was impracticable. Light ships were also invaluable for reconnaissance and communications. There had been many occasions during the civil wars on which Augustus was left in no doubt as to the value of sea power in securing the routes which controlled main supplies. It was Agrippa who became in effect the architect of the Imperial Navy with the establishment of the first permanent naval base at Fréjus (Forum Iulii); later Augustus built bases in Italy at Misenum and Ravenna. As the needs of the Empire grew, so the fleet began to proliferate, and new squadrons were raised. The *classis Moesica* was formed to patrol the lower Danube, the *classis Pannonica* the upper Danube, the Save and the Drave, and the *classis Pontica* the Black Sea. Clearly the lower Rhine would have needed a squadron, and this was created by Drusus the Elder, who had a canal cut between the Rhine and the Zuyder Zee to make a more direct contact with the North Sea. The conquest of Britain demanded a large force of transports. This in effect created the *classis Britannica*; there is evidence that skilled personnel were drafted from the Mediterranean. Once formed it became a permanent institution, and one finds along the south-east coast tiles stamped 'CL BR'. The internal organisation of the squadron with its many different kinds of ships, specialist shore officers, and craftsmen, made it the most complex branch of the whole army. As the recruitment at the end of the Republic was largely from the eastern Mediterranean, it is hardly surprising to find many of the titles were Greek, such as *trierarchus* and *navarchus*.

It would be interesting to know more about the ships of the British squadron. The war galleys designed for Mediterranean waters were notoriously unstable and, as Caesar discovered, much stouter ships were needed for the difficult waters of the Channel and the North Sea. That this problem must have been overcome is clearly demonstrated by the use made by Agricola of a squadron to circumnavigate the north coast of Britain. Perhaps the ships of the Veneti, whose ocean-going qualities showed up well in Caesar's Gallic and British campaigns, may have served as a model. How carefully the Romans of this period studied local conditions in constructing their transport vessels is seen in Tacitus' account of the preparations for Germanicus' expedition of A.D. 16.[14]

A thousand ships were thought to be adequate, and their construction was pushed ahead. Some were of shallow draught, pointed bow and stern, and broad-beamed to withstand heavy seas. Others were flat-bottomed to allow grounding. Most of them were equipped with steering-oars on both sides, to allow of quick movement forwards and backwards. Many had decks for the transport of artillery, horses and supplies. They were easy to sail, their oars gave them a turn of speed, and the keenness of their complement made them impressive and formidable.

III

What kind of opposition could the Roman Army expect to meet in Britain? The Belgic peoples of Britain, against whom they were soon to be engaged, were much akin to the Gauls and fought in the same manner. Body armour in the form of helmets and breast-plates was too expensive for any but the chiefs, their families, and their imme-diate entourage. The poorer Britons of the rank and file had little if any protection and, as Caesar relates, placed their reliance on magic. They painted their bodies with blue woad, probably in intricate patterns of curvilinear designs like the tattoo used by many primitive peoples today. The object was not only to provide protection through sacred symbols and ritual, but also by their very appearance to strike terror into their opponents. Since Caesar's day the Britons may have been softened by the introduction of luxury goods from the Roman world, but there had probably been much fighting in the conquests of Cunobelinus. Plautius could not expect an easy victory over tribesmen lured into a more civilised way of life. The Britons still put their faith in an instrument of war that had long been abandoned elsewhere—the chariot. The popular view of this vehicle is seen in the 'Boadicea' statue on the Embankment, where the British queen is shown riding in a solid-looking cart similar to those still seen on roundabouts at fun fairs. The Celtic chariot was quite different, and the way in which it was used is vividly portrayed by Caesar. He had first seen British chariots in action during the first invasion, and showed interest in this unusual method of warfare by giving a brief description of its technique:

> In chariot fighting the Britons begin by driving all over the field hurling javelins, and generally the terror inspired by the horses and

the noise of the wheels is sufficient to throw their opponents' ranks into disorder. Then, after making their way between the squadrons of their own cavalry, they jump down from the chariots and engage on foot. In the meantime their charioteers retire a short distance from the battle and place the chariots in such a position that their masters, if hard pressed by numbers, have an easy means of retreat to their own lines. Thus they combine the mobility of cavalry with the staying-power of infantry, and by daily training and practice they attain such proficiency that even on a steep incline they are able to control the horses at full gallop, and to check them in a moment. They can run along the chariot pole, stand on the yoke, and get back into the chariot as quick as lightning.[15]

The vehicle suitable for these rapid manœuvres would need to be very light and open at both ends. If more of the Arch of Claudius had survived there is little doubt that it would have shown examples among the trophies. Reconstruction has only been possible through the discovery of pieces of metalwork such as the wheels, hub caps, and other fittings. Some of these, found in Anglesey during the last war,[16] enabled Sir Cyril Fox to attempt a convincing reconstruction,[17] and a model of this can now be seen in the National Museum of Wales (7). It is a small square vehicle with wicker-work sides open at both ends to allow the warrior either to leap out at the back or run along the pole to the front and engage the enemy in single combat. This is, essentially, a kind of fighting designed for the aristocratic warrior. Fast streams of chariots could move swiftly along an unprotected flank, sting it with volleys of javelins, and escape before pursuit could be mounted. The chariots could also bring the warriors rapidly to any part of the battle needing their aid. The warriors would run out on foot, drive back the foe, and then retire to their vehicles, to be removed from the scene with speed and efficiency. It was ideal for open warfare where the heroic swordsman could show his prowess; against the Romans it could never be more than a novelty and annoyance.

IV

It can be no part of the plan of this book to narrate the details of Caesar's two British expeditions: still less,[18] to reopen any of the unsolved problems which they present. They concern us only for purposes of comparison. In A.D. 43, what lessons did they contain for Roman invaders and British defenders? And what light does their history throw for us on the diplomatic and military events of almost a century later than Caesar? These expeditions can, of course, only be understood in their context. It has been pointed out how they fall into place with Pompey's campaigns against the peoples of the Caucasus, and with Caesar's own crossing of the Rhine in that same summer of 55 B.C., to impress the tribes of western Germany with the power and reach of Rome. All derive from a technique for dealing with peoples on the fringe of the Empire, which might or might not lead to annexation as the next stage.[19] That personal reasons as well as public policy prompted Caesar in the British invasion of 55 B.C. is not to be doubted.[20] He believed Gaul to be pacified: yet he needed to justify the extension of his military command which he had gained at the Conference of Luca in 56 B.C. On the other hand, Caesar had just been engaged in a great struggle with the Belgic peoples of Gaul; he knew that they had kinsmen in Britain, and knew, or at least claimed to know, that support, moral and direct, had been sent to Gaul by these people for use against him. Yet he could get virtually no information about Britain of the kind a Roman governor of Gaul would need to know. The Gaulish merchants, assembled for interrogation, could or would disclose nothing. And Caesar himself had all but wiped out the Veneti, who had for so long been the most active in the British trade.

So it is that the British invasion of 55 B.C. is presented by Caesar as a reconaissance in force. There was, even so, a preliminary phase of diplomacy, but the Kentish tribes learned of his plans and sent delegates to promise submission—no doubt in the hope of persuading him to call off the invasion. Caesar—well informed by now of barbarian psychology—merely told them to persist with this admirable intention, and to confirm it by sending hostages. Then he sent them back to Britain, accompanied by his own diplomatic agent, Commius, King of the Atrebates. Commius, at this stage a faithful friend of Caesar's, yet a man of authority on either side of the Channel, played a vital role in both expeditions. Meanwhile Caesar had sent out Gaius Volusenus on a warship to collect what military information he could. That officer did not succeed in landing in Britain, but by offshore observation presumably surveyed the coast for some distance on either side of Dover.

The start was delayed, and it was not until August 25th that Caesar sailed from Boulogne with the VIIth and Xth Legions. The cavalry were to embark separately, probably from Ambleteuse: in the event storms prevented them from ever landing in Britain, a damaging blow to the success of the whole operation. The Kentish chiefs, having failed to forestall invasion, now decided to oppose it. Their forces, occupying strong positions on the heights above Dover, looked so menacing that Caesar moved north-east along the coast, to find an open beach between Walmer Castle and Deal. Even so, it was an awkward landing-place in the face of opposition. The ships could not put in close ashore: there were no landing-craft: the legionaries were understandably nervous about leaping into the sea and wading ashore through enemy fire. Only the famous standard-bearer of the Xth (fit comrade of that American sergeant on the Argonne—'Come on, do you want to live for ever?'), only he, and the effective use of Roman artillery from the ships, managed to get the troops to land. Once the legionaries were on the beach and able to draw up in battle-order, the Britons were routed, but lack of cavalry prevented any effective pursuit. Again British policy changed: there was renewed talk of submission and hostages: preparations were made for a meeting between Caesar and the chiefs. This edifying event never took place. The moon was full and the spring tides were due: they coincided with the great storm that had blown the cavalry transports back to Gaul. The consequences for Caesar's ships—warships and transports alike—were disastrous. Twelve out of rather more than seventy were a total loss, others were waterlogged or badly damaged. Caesar's force was now on an enemy shore without transport or supplies.

Troops should not be in such a position, and good commanders do not put them there. It was the hour of opportunity for the Britons and they did not fail to take it. A party of the VIIth Legion, out to forage corn, fell into a cleverly baited trap and was very roughly handled by that combination of cavalry and chariot-fighting that the Britons employed with such skill. Only Caesar's intervention saved them, and even he could do no more than escort them back to camp. A few days later a major British assault was delivered on the camp itself. It was beaten off by the legionaries, but again there was no pursuit. By now the autumn equinox was near and Caesar was anxious to be gone: all the Britons wanted was to have him out. It suited both sides to talk peace and arrange for hostages—no need actually to deliver them. As soon as the weather turned fair Caesar was off: those few fine autumn days were the only piece of good luck that came his way on this first expedition to Britain. Before a critical audience, in Gaul and Britain, his tactics had been ill-conceived in plan and slap-dash in execution. A blot had been made on his military reputation that would have to be erased. As for the Kentish chiefs, they could pass a happy winter, if they did not choose to look too far ahead. They had seen off the greatest Roman commander of his day. At one reaction, at least, we do not have to guess. For this mishandled affair the Roman Senate decreed a public thanksgiving for the unprecedented period of twenty days. The name of Mafeking is a reminder of the hysteria that can greet a military exploit of no great significance; again, the resolution of the Senate may, in part, be no more than a tribute to the efficiency of Caesar's political agents. But it also reflects, unmistakably, the Roman feeling about the remoteness of Britain, of the unknown hazards of the Ocean, and of the audacity of a commander who could dare this great military adventure.

The expedition of 54 B.C. was an altogether different story. Caesar took an adequate force—five legions, and 2,000 cavalry. He left in early July, with plenty of time for campaigning. But the storms of the great Gallic uprising were gathering, and he had to leave a further three legions and 2,000 cavalry to guard Boulogne and his communications with Rome; he also took to Britain a large number of Gallic nobles as hostages. He had got together an enormous fleet—more than 800 vessels of all descriptions, including many of his own design for conditions in the Channel. But he had made no effort to find a better landing-place than last year: indeed, south-westerly winds carried him up towards the North Foreland, and he had a hard row back with the tide to reach the open beaches a little north of his intended point, and probably between Sandown Castle and Sandwich. This time there was no contested landing—the mere sight of the great Roman fleet had overawed the British forces and caused them to disperse. Once ashore, Caesar acted with the speed that brought him so many victories: leaving only ten cohorts to guard the beach-head and the ships he made a night march towards the Stour, where he knew the Britons were concentrated in force. British cavalry and charioteers disputed the Stour crossing in a battle shortly after dawn; they then fell back to the *oppidum* of Bigbury, which was to fall to the assault of the VIIth Legion by late afternoon. But before he had been on British soil for forty-eight hours, Caesar was made aware of the horrors of British weather. A great storm arose on the second night of the invasion, causing havoc to the Roman fleet, and wrecking, this time, forty ships. Ten days work, carried on by night and day, were needed to beach the ships, carry out repairs, and extend the fortifications of the base-camp to enclose them. In the meantime, the military position on the British side had changed. The Kentish tribes had entrusted their cause to Cassivellaunus, chief of the Catuvellauni, whose capital was perhaps at Wheathampstead, near St Albans. (They may, indeed, have done this earlier, but Caesar did not find it out until the next stage of the campaign.) From this point a rational and effective strategy begins to make itself felt on the British side. When Caesar was once more able to drive inland, the enemy were ready to meet him on the Stour positions. British cavalry and charioteers, skilfully combined, harassed the Roman cavalry on the march. In a brisk action fought outside the Roman camp they impressed Caesar with their mobility and dash. The next day saw three legions and all the Roman cavalry in action on ground chosen by Caesar: this time the Roman cavalry finally swept the Britons from the field with heavy loss. Caesar is at pains to note that this was the last time Cassivellaunus was able to meet him in full strength. The passage implies, though it does not state, that Cassivellaunus commanded the British confederacy in person in these encounters. Though not victorious, he had other cards to play. The first was to dispute the passage of the Thames. What Caesar calls the only possible ford (Brentford? Coway Stakes?) had been protected on the north bank by *chevaux-de-frise* of sharp stakes, above and below water. A large British force was ready to

33

engage beyond this barrier. But a force of Roman cavalry got across upstream, and the legionaries waded the river and advanced with such *élan* that the Britons fell into the panic that overtakes those whose trusted line of defence has failed. Cassivellaunus now turned to guerrilla tactics, dismissing all his forces except for 4,000 charioteers, harassing the Roman line of march, driving away cattle and destroying supplies. He was thus able to restrict Caesar's movements, but not to prevent him from reaching Wheathampstead.

This massive earthwork has been confidently claimed as the stronghold of Cassivellaunus by its discoverer, Sir Mortimer Wheeler.[21] It lies near Verulamium, which became the capital of the Catuvellauni before the move to Camulodunum, and this fact alone makes the claim more than possible. The only other candidate is the Belgic *oppidum* at Gatesbury, some ten miles to the north-east, unless there are other sites of this nature awaiting discovery elsewhere in Hertfordshire. There is no conclusive proof to link Cassivellaunus and Caesar with Wheathampstead, but its situation, extremely large defences, and enormous size, all make the suggestion most plausible. At one point on the west side the defence ditch is over a hundred feet across, and, although the boundary of the fortress on the north side has yet to be defined, the *oppidum* could extend over as much as a hundred acres. The pottery found in the excavations would also fit this period; and, as Sir Mortimer has indicated, the Belgae were the first people to penetrate this area, which must for prehistoric settlement be classed as marginal land, difficult to clear and cultivate without the iron tools of quantity and quality introduced into Britain by these new immigrants. It is significant that Cassivellaunus was successful in drawing the Roman army into this difficult country and continually harassing it without Caesar discovering the existence or site of the *oppidum*. It was not until he had this vital information from the emissaries of the Trinovantes that he was able to launch an attack. Had the Celtic tribes presented a united front to the enemy, Caesar might have found himself in serious difficulties.

An attack by two legions captured the *oppidum*, with many prisoners and cattle, but Cassivellaunus and his main fighting strength got away. The British confederacy still held together: at Cassivellaunus' command the Kentish forces made a bold but unsuccessful attack on

Caesar's base-camp, with the objective, presumably, of destroying his ships. If this had succeeded, Caesar would have indeed been in trouble: it would have been more than a *quid pro quo* for the loss of Wheathampstead. But it failed, and Caesar's successes were beginning to attract some British tribes to his allegiance. Five small tribes, whose territories we do not know, had surrendered before the fall of Wheathampstead: more important, the powerful Trinovantes, foes to the Catuvellauni, had sought Caesar's protection and asked him to give them a ruler. And a ruler was to hand in their prince Mandubracius, who had been driven out by Cassivellaunus and sought refuge with Caesar in Gaul. Here was an agent for the advance of Roman influence in Britain as opportunity arose. Meanwhile the summer was passing: Gaul was becoming ever more restless: a negotiated peace suited both Caesar and Cassivellaunus. Caesar, of course, represents the initiative as coming from the British King: the fact that Commius was used as intermediary suggests that this was not so. Hostages were demanded, naturally: tribute was imposed and the annual amounts of payment laid down. Cassivellaunus was strictly required to leave Mandubracius and the Trinovantes alone. But Cassivellaunus retained his kingdom, and we do not know whether the tribute was ever paid. Then Caesar led his forces back to the Channel coast. Troops and prisoners necessitated two crossings to Gaul. Once again storms intervened. The ships that returned empty, together with sixty ships Labienus had constructed as reinforcement, mostly failed to appear. Caesar had to crowd his men together for the final crossing, shortly before September 21st. Luckily the weather was calm and none of the transports was lost. He was not destined to see Britain again. Vercingetorix, the Civil War, the Dictatorship, were to fill the ten years that were left before the Ides of March.

Whether a British province had a place in that great file of unfinished projects left by Caesar's death we cannot say—nor, if it had, how high a priority it might have held. He had shown that such a province might be set up, in the south-east of Britain at least, if it were thought worth while to do so, and provided that Gaul was pacified. Tacitus' verdict is a fair one, that Caesar 'can be seen to have shown it [Britain] to his successors, rather than to have made it over to them as a possession'. Yet, after all, how little Caesar had really learned about Britain can be judged from the three chapters (*De Bello Gallico*, v, 12–14) which he devoted to its geography and peoples. Short as they are, they contain a great deal of misinformation, much of which is unfortunately still reproduced in popular accounts of early British society. On the military side, sundry lessons emerge. The first is the importance of cavalry in any future Roman invading force: without them the legions would be vulnerable and seriously restricted. Caesar had shown that a balanced force of infantry and cavalry, well-handled, could sweep the Britons from the battlefield. Even more important was the need for a good land-locked harbour offering secure anchorage. Oceanus had intervened three times to protect the island and twice his intervention had been nearly fatal. For the Britons, the lessons of the two invasions need not have been wholly discouraging. The Roman army might be irresistible in the field, but guerrilla tactics could be used against it with good effect. And there was much more room for guerrilla tactics in Britain than the Romans yet knew. Above all, Caesar himself had twice invaded Britain, and twice sailed back to Gaul—the second time, never to return. When, three generations later, the Roman challenge was renewed, it is not surprising that the vastly stronger Belgic states of that time should feel that, if they could emulate their ancestors in valour, they too might win freedom for another hundred years.

Britain
on the
Eve of Invasion

2

In Britain political affairs at the invasion were fluid as they had not been for a generation. The death of the great King Cunobelinus in or about A.D. 40 removed the dominant figure whose shrewd and aggressive policy had built up a powerful Belgic Empire in south-east Britain, with its capital at Camulodunum (to use the Latin form of the name).[1] It stretched in a wide arc on either side of the Thames estuary, reaching Northamptonshire and the lands of the Coritani on the north-west, pressing hard on the frontier of the Iceni by Cambridge and Newmarket. Beyond the Thames it included northern Kent, the first lands of Belgic settlement; to the south-west it had made inroads into the kindred Belgic realm of the Atrebates—the former kingdom of Commius—in Berkshire and west Surrey. Trade and dynastic marriage had carried its influence more widely still. Among the Dobunni in the Cotswolds it seems that the state ruled from Bagendon was politically subordinate to the Belgae. The friendships and enmities aroused by this great expansion of Belgic power, though we cannot always trace them in detail, are the key to the course of the Roman invasion and to the intensive diplomacy that must have preceded it.

Economically and politically, this Belgic realm was the most advanced state in Britain. Their heavy plough and new tools made for the exploitation of richer soil than the light uplands farmed by the other British tribes. This in turn led to a denser population and a powerful army, for the Belgae had not lost the prowess of their continental ancestors, who resisted German invaders from across the Rhine and gave Caesar much hard fighting. But their main strength lay in their political organisation. These Belgae had crossed from Gaul in tribal units, preserving their identity and cohesion. Indeed, the main body of the Catuvellauni appears to have migrated to Britain, leaving only a remnant in their ancestral land round Châlons on the Marne. In Britain, the royal house of the Catuvellauni had produced three great rulers—Cassivellaunus, Tasciovanus, and Cunobelinus —who between them virtually spanned the century from the invasion of Caesar to that of Claudius. These men tolerated no factious, semi-independent nobles such as those who sapped the power of other British states; if there were quarrels, they were within the royal house, and there is no sign of them before Cunobelinus' old age.

Trade further strengthened an economy founded on agriculture and war. From the Channel ports and from the Thames estuary there was easy access to the continent and the rapidly expanding market of Roman Gaul. Camulodunum became an entrepôt for the exchange of the luxury goods of the Mediterranean world—wine, pottery, metal-work, ivory and amber—with the corn, cattle, leather, gold and slaves that the Empire was willing to purchase from Britain. Strabo[2] is at pains to stress that the customs' dues collected from these British exports produced more revenue than would accrue if the island were a province. The statement is, no doubt, an *apologia* for Augustus' failure to adopt a forward policy toward Britain. It also gives what we may take to be the official view of the force that would be needed to hold it if it were a Roman province, 'one legion and some cavalry'—a remarkable underestimate.

Yet archaeology warns not to exaggerate the civilisation of the Belgic realm. The excavations at Camulodunum reveal nothing that could be termed a city in the Greco-Roman sense of the word. Its most striking feature, indeed, is the complex series of earthen dykes by which it was defended, as part of a defensive system that includes the whole of the Colchester peninsula some twelve square miles in extent. The Sheepen site represents only a tiny fraction of this, about a quarter of a square mile, and although there were indications of the presence of a mint, and of sacred areas,[3] it is by no means certain whether this is the Belgic settlement which contained the residence of King Cunobelinus. There may be other and more important sites waiting discovery to the east or to the south. The excavations of 1930 to 1939 were instigated as a rescue operation in advance of the construction of the Colchester by-pass. Unfortunately the later Roman occupation of the site had seriously interfered with

6   *A Gallic warrior (Avignon Museum)*

7   *A reconstructed model of a British chariot*

8   *Celtic arms and equipment*
Detail of the Triumphal Arch at Orange

the earlier structures but the dwelling-places were huts of simple construction, round or sub-rectangular in plan. There were no signs of any elaborate timber work and the conclusion was reached that the smaller kind of Belgic dwelling was 'a structurally primitive and squalid hovel'. The only mitigation was the discovery of fine pottery imported from Gaul, which must have graced the boards of the local aristocracy but there was little glass or metalware. The nature of the place is, indeed, suggested by its Celtic name—Camulodunon 'the fort of Camulos'—the war-god who was the patron divinity of the royal house of the Catuvellauni. It cannot be denied that, so far, he had served his votaries well during their stay in Britain.

Aggressive though it was within the island, the policy of Cunobelinus towards Rome had always been correct and circumspect. True, nothing is heard of the tribute which Caesar had exacted from Cassivellaunus. But this seems to have soon been dropped—if indeed it was ever paid. In Cunobelinus' time it probably suited both sides to forget it. The Belgic king would have found it distasteful as a sign of submission; non-payment may also have suited Rome, for it would be a useful card to keep in reserve against some diplomatic occasion, when the demand could be presented, with arrears. When Roman soldiers were wrecked on the British coast in the great North Sea storm, they were punctiliously returned. There is no sign of meddling in Gallic politics while Cunobelinus held a firm grasp of power. But the history of Wales and Scotland provides many examples of the fatal flaw that became apparent in Celtic society when a great king approached his end, and the quarrel for succession broke out among his sons. How many sons Cunobelinus had is unknown. There cannot have been less than five—Togodumnus, Caratacus, Adminius, and the 'brothers' mentioned by Tacitus as present at the time of Caratacus' final defeat. Nothing is known of the details of the quarrel between them, only its sequel, the expulsion of Adminius and his flight to the Emperor Gaius in A.D. 39.[4]

The Belgic Empire was now divided between Togodumnus and Caratacus. The evidence suggests—though it does not prove—that Togodumnus ruled an eastern kingdom from Camulodunum, while Caratacus took the newly-won land in the south-west, with his capital at Calleva, the old centre of the Atrebates. Both were proud

Celtic princes and good generals, by the standards prevailing in Britain. Both were heirs to the imperialist tradition of their house; both shared, untempered by prudence, the anti-Roman feeling endemic for more than a century among the Belgae.

The evidence for expansion of the Belgic kingdom in the few years between Cunobelinus' death and the Claudian invasion is scanty. None the less, something can be made of the few brief references in Tacitus, Suetonius, and Dio, when they are interpreted in the light of expert analysis of the coinage of the British tribes.[5] Most of the expansion, it is clear, was the work of Caratacus. Tacitus speaks of him as 'ruling many peoples'. He is represented by two coins only (one of them doubtful), but these are in the Silchester region,[6] and it seems likely that from this base he was pushing west and south-west. A western thrust would bring him to the lands of the Dobunni, to that Cotswold area round the *oppidum* at Bagendon which bears archaeological evidence of subjection to the Catuvellauni. And, to the south-west, he would encroach further on the old Atrebatic realm that had been divided up amongst Commius' sons. There are here the coins of a certain Verica, who probably ruled at Selsey Bill, a site now under the sea, and there seems little doubt that this is the 'Bericus' mentioned by Dio[7] as taking refuge with Claudius, and providing the diplomatic excuse for Roman intervention. The stock-piling of such refugees for use if required was well-tried in Roman diplomacy. It had been used on a grand scale on the Eastern frontier with claimants and pretenders to the thrones of Parthia and Armenia. Later Agricola was to receive an Irish chieftain 'expelled by domestic strife', and keep him against an emergency.[8] Now that there were two refugees, Adminius and Bericus, in Claudius' hands, one with a claim to the old Belgic realm, the other to part of its newest conquests, it was natural enough for Togodumnus and Caratacus to demand their return, though how to interpret the armed demonstration which followed (*Britanniam tunc tumultuantem*)[9] is hard to say. Some have read into the phrase the improbable idea of an attack on the Channel coast of Gaul; this seems to postulate more naval strength than the Belgae are known to have possessed. More likely they continued to harass states friendly to Rome, whose appeals for aid would finally tip the balance in favour of invasion.

44

II

The other British states were far less formidable entities. Divided and broken, the old realm of Commius can only have been a secondary target for the invasion. A portion of it, that ruled from Venta (Winchester) and including the Isle of Wight, seems to have retained both its political freedom and the anti-Roman feelings that Commius had brought with him from Gaul. Much the same may have been true of the north-western realm, in north Wiltshire and the Somerset fringe, though here the picture is obscure. It certainly applied to the Durotriges, a warlike though loosely-knit people whose territory stretched from western Hampshire into east Devon. These coastal lands also gave a home to many refugees from Gaul, whose elaborate hill-forts were the most formidable of their kind in Britain. Hambledon, Hod Hill, Cadbury Castle, Maiden Castle and the rest—the Ordnance Survey Map of Iron Age Britain shows well over twenty multivallate forts of more than fifteen acres in the known territory of the tribe. These are the forts of powerful, independent chiefs, under little if any control from a common overlord, and trying to maintain themselves in a world of warring neighbours. In context and purpose they are like the marcher castles of Wales. Time has denuded them now to their earthworks, but even so they are among the most impressive monuments in Britain as they look from height to height across the wide green landscape of Wessex. It will remain for a later chapter to consider the military problems that they posed.

The states so far described were, in the event, to provide the main opposition to the Roman conquest of south-east Britain. But the Belgic and Belgicising peoples were ringed by uneasy neighbours, potentially friendly to Rome, or at least non-aligned. In Sussex and the Weald a people whose ethnic name we do not know (later they were part of the kingdom of the Regnenses) were menaced by the expansion of the Catuvellauni into Kent and over the Atrebates. In their large hill-forts along the South Downs—Cissbury, Devil's Dyke, Caburn, and others—they maintained as yet their independence. To them the Roman invasion must have seemed a welcome prospect, and one may suppose that they were ready to act as a bridge-head if required. The Iceni of Norfolk and Suffolk were

9 Iron Age tribes and sites to which reference is made

in like case. They had more room for manœuvre, and may well have been a more powerful tribe, but shortly before A.D. 43 they seem to have lost their border outposts on the Gogs south of Cambridge,[10] and to have retreated northwards through the Newmarket gap between the forest and the Fens. West of the Durotriges, the Dumnonii held the whole peninsula of Devon and Cornwall. Their hill-forts are smaller and less elaborate than those of Wessex, some of them being of the promontory type common in, e.g., Brittany. Except for the high land of Dartmoor and Exmoor, settlement seems to have been extensive; it was dense in western Cornwall. From Ictis in Mounts Bay, and probably from other ports, there was trade with Brittany. There is no sign of a strong central control and not much, later, of hostility to the Roman advance. The position is more complicated with the wealthy tribe of the Dobunni. Possessed of the good agricultural lands of the Cotswolds and of the mineral resources of Dean (perhaps of Mendip?), minting coins and ruled by powerful kings, theirs was a more advanced culture than that of their kin in Dumnonia. But shortly before the Roman invasion they became divided into a south-eastern and a north-western realm, and the latter seems to have fallen tributary to the rulers of Camulodunum.

Hill-forts of the Wessex type extend up the Wye and Severn valleys as far as Old Oswestry and Llanynymech Hill. The hills are higher and bolder on this mountainous fringe of Wales, and there is a dramatic quality to such sites as Herefordshire Beacon, Malvern, and Croft Ambrey near Ludlow. Tribal boundaries are uncertain, but the heartlands of the Cornovii were in Shropshire and Cheshire, and their centre may well have been the Wrekin.[11] Settlement must have been thin on the high Midland plateau, but crop-marks of farm-steads are dense along the river terraces with their light subsoils. Eastwards again lay a belt of liass and oolite more suitable for agriculture. Here lay the lands of the Coritani, stretching from the Warwickshire Avon to the Lincoln Wolds and perhaps the Humber. Their position exposed them to Belgic pressure from the south-east, and archaeological evidence suggests that a Belgic dynasty ruled from a site near Sleaford on the eve of the invasion. Beyond Humber and Mersey the Brigantes, a confederacy of warlike peoples, held the

Pennine and Cumbrian moors and mountains under the uneasy rule
of a monarchy. In what is now the East Riding of Yorkshire the
Parisii seem to have maintained intact the tribal identity they had
brought to Britain from their Gallic homeland between the Seine and
the Marne. What is now Wales was divided between four main
tribes, whose territories correspond, roughly, to the four ancient
Welsh dioceses. The Demetae of the south-west are the least-known.
though in Dyfed they have left their tribal name on the land. But the
Silures of the south-east were to play a great part in resisting the
Roman conquest. Tacitus notes the physical characteristics that
marked them off from the other peoples of Britain, and speculates
about a possible Iberian origin.[12] The Plain of Gwent gave them a
good tract of agricultural land, and the Black Mountains and Brecon
Beacons a natural fortress. Mona (Anglesey) and the mountains of
Eryri played the same role for the Ordovices, whose fighting spirit
was enhanced by the presence in Mona of the headquarters of the
Druids. In Britain as in Gaul, this priesthood fostered pan-Celtic and
anti-Roman feeling. Between Conway and Dee were the Deceangli:
their hill-forts, of the Wessex type, stretch above the Clwydian range.
The name survives in Deganwy.

III

This survey has touched on all the British states involved in any way
in the Claudian conquest. It is to be noted that the invasion was preceded by an intensive phase of diplomacy, an arm which Rome
exploited against the barbarian peoples no less effectively than war.
On the Rhine and Danube frontiers in particular, dealing with military problems far more intractable than those of Britain, the cool
head and long experience of Tiberius had shown what could be done
by provoking and sustaining the enmities endemic among the tribes.
Tacitus shows this policy in action at a dramatic moment—in A.D. 16
immediately after Germanicus had won his great victory at the Battle
of Idistaviso. The Roman commander believed that the enemy were
flagging: 'one more summer in the field, and the German war could
be wound up'. But he kept getting letters from Tiberius advising
him to return and celebrate the Triumph already voted.

We have had enough [said the Emperor] of successes and disasters. You have won great victories, but you must also remember what the winds and waves have done—through no fault of the commander— to cause grievous and heavy loss. I was sent into Germany by Augustus nine times, and I achieved more by diplomacy than by war. That was how the Sugambri surrendered, how the Suebi and King Maroboduus were induced to keep the peace. As for the Cherusci and the other bellicose tribes, the vengeance of Rome has been duly provided for. Now we can leave them to quarrel among themselves.

No Roman could speak out of a fuller knowledge of the peoples of northern Europe. He had seen their inveterate tendency to quarrel among themselves allow Rome to pass safely through the moment of supreme peril—when after the disaster to Varus in A.D. 9 the victorius Arminius had besought the Marcomanni to join him in a great offensive against Roman power. The barbarians could be relied upon to quarrel after a war, they could be softened up by diplomacy before it began.

So now, in Britain, offers of client kingship will have kept some British rulers out of the struggle. Strabo[13] tells us that British kings visited Augustus in Rome and made offerings in the Capitol which, as has been pointed out,[14] could only signify the ratification of treaties. Thus at least two of the British tribes had already entered into a relationship with Rome which may have lasted into the time of Claudius, and may have been recognised after A.D. 43 by the creation of client kingships for the Iceni and for Cogidubnus. The latter emerges as one of the leading Britons in the Roman province, but his place in the invasion and conquest must be considered later.

If the main terms were known in advance it explains why the Senate was prepared to allow Claudius *carte blanche* in ratifying the settlement of British affairs.[15] But the biggest piece on the board eluded the skill of the Roman negotiators. This was, of course, to force a breach between Togodumnus and Caratacus. A passage in Tacitus[16] suggests that it was tried, for in his speech before Claudius Caratacus refers to a period of success and prosperity, in which prudence on his part could have led to a treaty of friendship with Rome. The best context for such a proposition would be that of negotiations immediately before the invasion. But loyalty held between the

49

brothers, and they resolved to direct the united forces of their kingdoms against the Romans.

We are nowhere told how many men they were able to put into the
field, though some sort of estimate may be made. In the few weeks of
the campaign, their forces fought two holding operations, then a
two-day battle on the Medway against the full strength of the invading army, next a cavalry action after the Thames crossing, and
perhaps (though this is doubtful) a further action to dispute the
advance to Camulodunum. There still remained enough fighting men
for an effective force to follow Caratacus to Wales. The Medway
battle is the key. To hold up a Roman army of some 40,000 would
surely call for a British force substantially larger, of at least 60,000
men. It is not extravagant to suppose that the Belgic princes could
mobilise 80,000 men or more. This in turn would suggest a population of at least 400,000 from which they could be drawn, according
to the formula which no less an authority than Caesar used to estimate
Gallic population and resources.[17] Some comparisons may be helpful.
The Helvetii who invaded Gaul in 58 B.C. reckoned their total number, with their allies, at 368,000, of whom 90,000 were fighting men.
These were defeated by Caesar near Bibracte with an army of six
legions and auxiliaries. The great host mustered against him by the
Belgae in 57 B.C. was said by Gallic observers to number almost
300,000—a figure which has rightly provoked scepticism. With
40,000 men, and the advantage of carefully chosen ground, Caesar
was able to defeat them and cause them to disperse. At Neuf-Mesnil
the Nervii, most warlike of the Belgic peoples, gave Caesar's six
legions a desperate fight with an army of 60,000 men. Diodorus
Siculus, following Posidonius, says that the larger Gallic states could
field an army of about 200,000 men; the smaller, about 50,000.[18]
Like all ancient estimates of population, these figures can only be
accepted with caution. But they do give an order of magnitude, if not
an actual figure, and they do not suggest that the resources of Cunobelinus' realm were equal to those of the greater Gallic states of
Caesar's day.

Since the Belgic decision to oppose Rome led to military disaster
and the end of their kingdoms' independence, it is tempting to ask
why it ever seemed valid. Here again we may look to Tacitus. To the

British observer, Rome's record in north-western Europe might not seem impressive—at least, not since the victories of Julius Caesar. The disaster inflicted on Varus by Arminius in A.D. 9 had not really been erased by the prestige victories won by Germanicus. Augustus' advice to maintain the frontiers of the Empire as he had left them had been a realistic appraisal, loyally accepted by Tiberius. Gaius' attempt to breach it had been a fiasco. And who was Claudius, if not the most unmilitary of emperors? Again, the Britons were sustained by their own interpretation of the invasions of Julius Caesar. Tacitus makes Caratacus, and later Boudicca, invoke the memory of Caesar's defeat and withdrawal from the island.[19] The delay before the troops of Claudius could be got to embark must have encouraged the belief that invasion was not seriously intended; the appeal to the deeds of their ancestors, that it could be defeated. A credible picture could be built up, by men not naturally gifted at reckoning the odds. Tacitus, Caesar, and Livy all emphasise the recklessness of the Celts in pitting themselves against danger, and their irresolution once it had come. One thinks of Bituitus, the great king of the Arverni, watching with confidence the armies of Domitius Ahenobarbus and Fabius Maximus moving to battle positions. 'They are too few to feed my hounds!' was his contemptuous remark.[20] They were enough to win the battle that secured for Rome a permanent hold on Southern Gaul. The *audacia* of Caratacus and Togodumnus was of a different order, but proceeded from the same cause: the determination of brave men to defend their freedom without counting too closely the cost.

No classical writer discusses at any length the Roman motives for the invasion. The fact is significant: it was not thought to require elaborate justification. This has not deterred modern scholars from propounding numerous and conflicting theories,[21] the need to exploit British minerals, to complete the Romanisation of Gaul, to suppress Druidism, to break up the dangerous concentration of military strength along the Rhine, to win personal glory for Claudius, and so on. Armed with the knowledge of hindsight, and in the light of the difficulties Rome encountered in the highland zone of Britain and of her ultimate failure in Scotland, they have been inclined to doubt the wisdom of the whole British venture. To argue thus is to ignore the situation of A.D. 43 and the objectives at which the invasion itself was aimed. Julius Caesar's British expeditions had bequeathed to his successors an unfinished task. He had set up a simulacrum of Roman authority in south-east Britain that had failed to produce results. Augustus had shown a wish to come to grips with the problem, but had been distracted. Tiberius had followed his advice not to advance the Imperial frontiers. The abortive plans of Gaius had led to a dangerous loss of prestige. Now, with the death of Cunobelinus and the quarrels among his sons, the time was ripe to secure a Roman hold on the most civilised and the most dangerous part of the island by reducing the Belgic Empire to a Roman Province. Seen in this light, the Claudian invasion appears to have aimed at a limited objective and promised a valuable return.

The Invasion
and the Defeat
of the Belgic Kingdom

3

Any account of the invasion must begin with a recognition of the sketchy nature of the historical sources. The episode will have been treated at length by Tacitus in the *Annals*, but the books dealing with the years A.D. 37–47 are missing. The loss is irreparable. The only continuous narrative we have is that of Dio Cassius—a very inferior substitute.[1] Dio wrote in the early third century—nearly two hundred years after the invasion—and we do not know and cannot evaluate the sources he used. Two inscriptions, one from the Arch of Claudius in Rome, the other from the contemporary arch at Cyzicus, give a brief but invaluable glimpse of the official line.[2] Two paragraphs of Suetonius' *Lives* (*Claudius* and *Vespasian*) offer marginal and anecdotal information.[3] Archaeological evidence amplifies some points, but to a less extent than could be wished. Such are the narrow limits within which we must work.

Embarkation accomplished, the Roman command could put into operation their plans for the next phase. Two hazards confront the invader of Britain—the fight in the Channel and the opposed landing. It seems to us natural that the islanders should muster whatever fleet they maintain and engage the invader at sea. When that fleet disposes of formidable striking power, the invader may never dare to leave the coasts of the continent. This is what pinned down Napoleon's troops at Boulogne. The invasion-barges and warships that Hitler had assembled seemed a menace through the long and terrible weeks of the late summer of 1940, but it was a menace that never materialised. The fate of the Spanish Armada is a signal example of what may be in store for the invader: *afflavit Deus et dissipati sunt*. But William of Normandy crossed unopposed, and the prospect of a naval engagement was not one of the anxieties of Aulus Plautius. For the last 'native' sea-power in these waters had been that of the Veneti, defeated by Caesar. No other was to appear until the ships of the Saxons challenged the *classis Britannica* under Carausius in the late third century, or those of King Niall of the Nine Hostages cruised in the Irish Sea and the English Channel in the fourth. Had Cunobelinus anticipated Alfred in raising a fleet . . . but such a venture was far beyond the horizon of any of the British states.

The opposed landing was another matter. No commander, ancient or modern, has relished the idea of landing his forces in the teeth of enemy opposition. Notoriously, Caesar's first expedition to Britain (55 B.C.) had run into serious difficulties on this very point. The famous standard bearer of the Xth Legion, leaping into the sea and calling on his men to follow, was an episode more edifying to read about than to see repeated.[4] How to avoid an engagement on these terms must have been a major problem for the staff tacticians. Dio's statement that the Roman force sailed in three divisions is a pointer to their solution. This was done, he says, 'to avoid the hindrance in landing that might delay a single force'. Would this hindrance come from the beach-head selected, inadequate for so large a force? Or from the enemy? The latter seems more likely. In their appreciation of the problem, the Roman staff must have assumed that a strong British force would be maintained along the coast. A general alarm once given, the Britons would prepare to defend the beaches. But if a decoy force could be used to deceive the Britons as to Roman intentions, an unopposed landing might be possible at the point selected for the main attack. The care with which this selection was made does credit to the Roman staff-work, for they discovered by far the best possible place. The key to it is the Wantsum Channel, then a broad navigable channel separating Thanet from the mainland. At its southern entrance and off the western shore lay a sizeable island, site of the later Rutupiae, and of a Saxon Shore fort. Even in the drained landscape of today it is conspicuous across the flats from Sandwich, rising as it does fifty-eight feet above sea-level. In Roman times a navigable channel came up to its eastern side, and it offered an area of dry ground for the safe unloading of men and stores. Once this was secured, other factors would come into play. The Wantsum Channel itself was virtually a landlocked roadstead, and a long sand-spit running out from the southern point of Thanet would further protect the Richborough anchorage. Direct access to the Thames—at least at high tide—would make it unnecessary for ships to round the North Foreland. A British attack on the position would have to cross the channel to the west of the island in the face of Roman sea-power. On the mainland, a ridge of high ground would offer good going for a Roman thrust against the Canterbury area, where was in all likelihood the nearest main centre of British power. And finally, if the worst should happen, it would be possible for Aulus Plautius to draw off his troops and transports without undue loss. The search for a good beach-head has occupied many commanders at many periods of history, on both sides of the Channel. Seldom can a position have offered so many advantages to the invading forces as the island at Rutupiae.

Two other things emerge in Dio's account of the crossing. Contrary winds drove back the Roman Fleet, and the crossing was made at night as those of Caesar had been. 'They became disheartened at being driven back . . . but recovered their spirits when they saw a flash of light rise in the east and shoot across to the west—the direction of their course.' It is impossible to determine whether this night crossing was accidental—the result of headwinds—or deliberately planned. If the latter, the invasion scheme must have provided for the main force to embark in the late afternoon, cross the Channel under cover of darkness, and land in the early dawn.

Something of the anxieties of that night filter through into Dio's narrative. An invading army, sailing towards an enemy shore, is in a situation which concentrates the mind wonderfully—as Dr Johnson remarked of the man about to be hanged. Perhaps some of the officers, when they saw the bright flash, recalled that other meteor which had induced Anchises to leave Troy, launching Aeneas and his followers into their high destiny. The nervous tension of the troops was no doubt heightened by this portent, and they will have needed a steadying remark such as that produced by the Greek general Epaminondas on a similar occasion, and recorded by Frontinus. 'The heavenly powers have sent us this light.' Less famous and less striking than the appearance of Halley's comet which heralded the triumph of William of Normandy in 1066, the meteor of that late summer night of A.D. 43 none the less urged forward the invaders of Britain. Ahead of the fleet that evening of late summer lay the four hundred years of Roman Britain, the roads and the cities and the villas, the flames of Boudicca's rebellion, and the bitter years of fighting in the north. But soldiers do not have these long thoughts. Each man must have speculated on the unknown coastline that lay ahead, the enemy assault, and his own prospects in the fight on the beach.

II

The operation so far described called for two forces—main and decoy. The decoy force perhaps made a landfall by the cliffs of Dover and turned west to draw the Britons away from the main landing. What of the third force mentioned by Dio? For this one needs to consider the possibility of the Romans making a link with a force of British allies. As shown above, Roman diplomacy had skilfully maintained a foothold in Britain, and it could be established that there was a sound political justification for the invasion, since the Romans were coming to the aid of an ally. It is also certain that the principal ally was the tribe of the Atrebates, who held one of the best anchorages along the south-east coast at Bosham on Chichester harbour. Reviewing the events from the distance of many centuries, it would seem obvious strategy for the army to make this their main base of operations. But the Roman dislike of the sea and the considerable extra distance along the coast undoubtedly led to the use of the shorter crossing to Rutupiae and the Kentish harbours for the main force.

One of the key figures in this phase must have been the chieftain Cogidubnus, who eventually emerges as *rex et legatus Augusti in Britannia*. These titles appear on an inscription found in Chichester in 1723, now built into the wall of the Town Hall (see Appendix II, p. 184). It records the building of a temple to Neptune and Minerva by the guild of smiths or metalworkers. The selection of deities suggests that the guild was closely connected with shipping; they may have been shipwrights or chandlers. The erection of such a building could hardly have taken place soon after the invasion as time must be allowed for the founding of the town and the development of its industries to the point when there was a guild wealthy enough to finance such an enterprise. Cogidubnus lived long enough for Tacitus to recall that he had been faithful to Rome 'till our own day', implying that the British king was still alive in the seventies.[5] The balance of probability is that this inscription must be dated to this late period and therefore it offers no proof that Cogidubnus received his title of *legatus Augusti in Britannia* from Claudius. Indeed it is hardly likely that Claudius would have done more than make him a Roman citizen and client king. The names Tiberius Claudius taken by Cogidubnus show that he owed this honour at least to Claudius, but the second title, that of Imperial Legate, is a different matter.[6] The words of Tacitus when he refers to Cogidubnus suggest that that monarch had occasion to demonstrate his loyalty at a later date, and it is not difficult to suggest an occasion. As will be seen below, the general responsible for the conquest of the south-west was Vespasian, and during his arduous campaign he would have needed bases in friendly hands. There is now archaeological evidence that one of these was probably in Bosham harbour not far from the new capital of Cogidubnus (Noviomagus, at Chichester). Vespasian would certainly have had a very close and amicable relationship with the British king, and the future Emperor was not a man to forget his old cronies. There was a time in the civil war of A.D. 68–9 when there was divided loyalty among the legions of Britain. As the star of Vespasian gained its ascendant the presence in Britain of an old friend and loyal supporter may have been critical in preventing the legions from joining the opposing side. Vitellius could muster only token forces from Britain and the Governor, Vettius Bolanus, prevaricated when pressed for more. If Cogidubnus had been active on behalf of Vespasian, here was a time when it could have been rewarded. Election to the Roman Senate at this time would have caused no eyebrows to be raised and the extraordinary title (which is difficult to explain in any other context) could be considered merely as a high honour to the King, now an old man. The title would have given equality with the Governor, in itself an awkward anomaly in any other circumstances.[7]

Another version of the events of this period has been presented.[8] This ingenious hypothesis introduces another character into the

SCALE IN FEET

0   200   400   600

outer ditch

inner ditch

entrance

RICHBOROUGH STREAM

R. STOUR

10   *The Claudian camp at Richborough*

situation—Cn. Sentius Saturninus, who had been consul in 41 and was a man of some importance, although junior to the new Governor, Aulus Plautius. He escapes mention in Dio but appears linked with Plautius in the brief account of the invasion given by the fourth-century historian Eutropius.[9] It is suggested that Sentius was given a diplomatic appointment and sent to Britain with Cogidubnus to meet the British kings and come to terms with them. The Briton would have been the negotiator fulfilling the role Commius did for Caesar in Britain in 55 B.C. Sentius Saturninus, with the powers of an Imperial Legate, could have signed treaties and given undertakings in an attempt to win over the wavering loyalties of some of the kings of Britain. The task completed, Cogidubnus—according to this theory—took over the titles held by Sentius Saturninus. It is a most attractive idea, but this is too weighty a superstructure to be built on the introduction of his name by Eutropius. It is known that a number of important senators accompanied Claudius to Britain as his *comites* or advisory council. Sentius Saturninus was a man of uncertain loyalty[10] and would have been too dangerous to leave behind in Rome. Thus a much more rational and simple explanation can be found.

There seems little doubt that Cogidubnus was of material assistance in the initial stages of the conquest; none that he was rewarded with citizenship and a kingdom. He may have acted as a negotiator on behalf of Plautius or he may have had command of a small force which landed at Bosham and operated on the long exposed flank of the Britons. He may even have secured the bridge over the Thames. Perhaps we shall never know the answer. But finds at Chichester attest the presence of legionaries at this period—whether they came at this stage of the advance or when the place was a base for operations under Vespasian in the same year it is quite impossible to decide. It would indeed be a most remarkable discovery that could distinguish between sites and objects so close together in time.

It is time to return to Richborough, which we have postulated as a key point for the invasion. Excavations have shown that, apart from traces of the Early Iron Age, the earliest occupation of the site was associated with Claudian coins, pottery and military equipment.[11]

The structural remains of this phase consist of two parallel V-shaped ditches of typical military profile with an entrance and causeway. These ditches were traced for a total length of 705 yards and there was definite evidence of a corner at the southern limit, but only a slight turn at the north end. The east side of the site is bounded by the River Stour and the Richborough stream, which flows through what is now a low-lying marshy area. Considerable physical changes have taken place on the seaward side, with the silting of the Wantsum Channel and the total disappearance of the Roman harbour. It is nevertheless doubtful if much land has been lost by encroachment or erosion; though the walls of the Saxon Shore fort on its east side have been undermined and fallen outwards, they may well have been built at the edge of the sea. In effect then, the area contained by the Claudian ditches was much the same as it is today—about ten acres. When the Roman Army camped, their leather tents were set out in orderly array at an approximate concentration of 250 men per acre. This landing base would therefore have held about 2,500 men, no more than a task force sent over to secure a bridge-head.

Bushe-Fox concludes from his examination of the ditches that they were in being for only a short time and states that 'the earthwork was without doubt formed as a temporary defence to cover the disembarkation of the troops at the time of the invasion and to serve as a protection for the ships drawn up on to the shore during the initial stages of the campaign in A.D. 43. There is no evidence of a heavy occupation at this period, and only a small detachment may have been in garrison there: it may even have been left derelict for several years.' If Richborough had been the main base surely more forces would have arrived and been accommodated. There is certainly enough room on the plateau to the west; if the camp of ten acres was an initial landing base for the task force, the ditches would have been quickly filled in and a much larger area taken over for 30–40,000 men. This would have required a camp of 120–160 acres. Very little excavation has been carried out beyond the area of the Saxon Shore fort[12] and it is possible that the defences of such a large camp may yet be found.

As soon as the army was established in Britain, the value of the

11 *Embarking men and supplies at a port*
From Trajan's Column in Rome

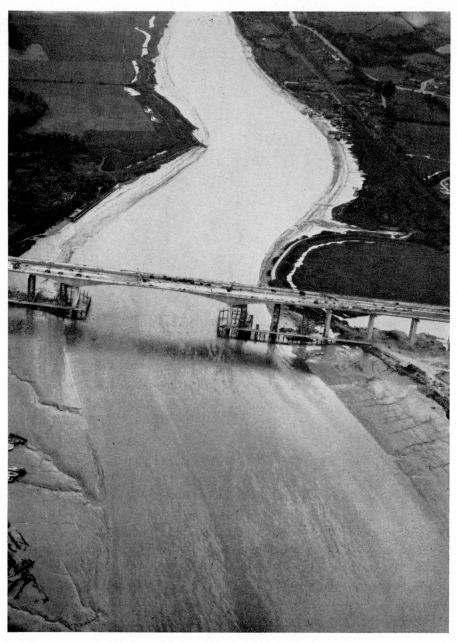

12 *The River Medway above Rochester, at the point where
the Roman army probably fought its way across*

land-locked harbour at Richborough became apparent. The next stage was the erection of a large store-base. Some of its timber buildings can be identified as granaries since their floors are built on a series of uprights, well above the ground level, with an air space between, thus avoiding the effect of damp and entry by small animals.[13] These buildings remained in position (according to the excavator) until *c*. A.D. 85, but they probably went out of use at a much earlier date, once supplies could have been taken to more convenient points nearer the military bases.

III

Wherever the landing—or landings—took place, the important fact is that they were unopposed. Not only that, but Plautius found no large British force in the vicinity. Dio tells us that the Britons were tired of waiting and had gone home. The delay caused by the refusal to embark had led to the dispersal of the British levies. The mutiny had been of benefit, after all. It would have been difficult for the Belgic chiefs to hold their men together for any length of time. There was no standing professional army; the only troops, apart from the aristocratic warriors and their personal followers, were the British farmers, taken from their unremitting tasks to wait for an army which never came. As the days and weeks went by and rumours of mutiny in the Roman Army were brought in, it is hardly surprising that the Belgic war-lords decided that there had been another fiasco, and yielded to the pressure of levies anxious to return to their farms and families.

This explains why Plautius 'had some difficulty in finding the Britons'. R. G. Collingwood conjured up a vivid picture of the harassed general marching and counter-marching up and down Kent with one eye on Caesar's commentaries and the other on the depopulated Kentish landscape.[14] This is over-imaginative. Plautius may have been surprised at the absence of Britons but he set about the very necessary task of establishing his base with its supplies while light units gently probed into Kent. Unlike Caesar he did not take advantage of the situation and rush boldly forward to seize points of strategic importance. It is probable that the tribes of east Kent rapidly came to terms with the Romans as soon as their strength and purpose was revealed.

Meanwhile the two leaders of the Belgae had not been idle. As soon as news reached them of the landing they decided on a strategy of reassembling their main armies at the Medway crossing, where the issue was to be decided. Doubtless with a view to delaying the Roman advance, at least two skirmishes were fought by the two brothers on separate occasions or places. Plautius, says Dio, first defeated Caratacus, then Togodumnus. Caratacus, if he had been ruling the south-western kingdom, would naturally make the first contact with the Romans. The fact that they were operating independently at this stage need not have been bad tactics if it was to shield the main build-up of strength behind them and to test the Roman strength.

Before the main battle a curious event is inserted—the capitulation of the 'Bodunni'. This episode has been subject to close study by Professor C. F. C. Hawkes and in a most ingenious and convincing line of argument he suggests that this was a levy of a section of the Dobunni from Gloucestershire.[15] The coin evidence now suggests that this tribe was divided into two parts. The northernmost had its headquarters at Bagendon near Cirencester, and the finds there indicate either a very strong trading and cultural relationship with the Catuvellauni, or, what seems more likely, their actual conquest. The southern part of the tribe occupying south Gloucestershire and north Somerset did not share the same degree of Belgic influence, and, as Professor Hawkes has argued, these peoples were probably descendants of a westward extension of the Atrebates. Had the northern part of the Dobunni been assimilated by Belgic culture, it is not likely that they would have been so eager to capitulate to Plautius; that they did so is suggestive of enslavement and enforced levies raised against Rome. Earlier historians attempted to involve Plautius in an invasion of the south-west, since Dio appears to state that a garrison was planted in 'their', i.e. Dobunnic, territory. Professor Hawkes argues that the Greek word *entautha* used by Dio need not mean this, but simply 'thereupon'. In other words, Plautius received this surrender and thereupon, leaving a garrison behind—the normal method of consolidating gains—continued his advance.

Next he came to a river. 'The barbarians thought that the Romans would not be able to cross it without a bridge and consequently bivouacked in a rather careless fashion on the opposite bank.' The only river which would fit these conditions in Kent is the Medway. The main route followed by the Roman Army was probably the ancient prehistoric trackway along the North Downs which was later to become famous as the Pilgrims' Way along which Chaucer's company rode to the shrine of Thomas à Becket at Canterbury. There are several crossing points of the river between Aylesford and Rochester, but most of them would have been suitable only for small parties with pack animals. The river below Aylesford pursues a winding course through marshy and wooded ground where access to its banks would have been difficult. The obvious crossing point for a large army would have been immediately above Rochester, where there is firm ground on both sides down to the river edge and excellent visibility along the river from the heights on the east bank. This is the point chosen by the engineers who have designed the course of the new Medway motorway, whose bridge almost straddles the ancient crossing. Here of course the river is tidal, and the ford may only have been usable at low tide; this may account for the time it took the Romans to secure their bridge-head. It should be added that the hill now occupied by Borstal would provide the Roman commander with an admirable grandstand view of the battlefield. A similar but more distant position is available for the British command on the west bank (*12*).

The Roman army may have had qualms about an opposed landing from the sea, but for river-crossings they were well trained and equipped. The section in Frontinus' *Stratagems* devoted to river-crossings concentrates on the element of surprise and outflanking manœuvres. Moreover, the Romans had specialist troops for just such an operation. These were the Frisian and Batavian cavalry regiments whose experience in the Low Countries had accustomed them to crossing such barriers and fighting in waterlogged terrain. We meet them in the *Annals* of Tacitus doing good service in Germanicus' northern campaigns, and they were to do even better in Britain in such operations as the crossing of the Menai Straits. Dio's account of the Medway operation is very sketchy:

He (Plautius) sent across Gallic troops who were trained to swim with full equipment across the swiftest of rivers. Surprise was achieved . . . by this attack: they did not shoot at the men themselves: instead, wounding the horses that drew their chariots, they made it impossible even for the charioteers to get away in the subsequent confusion. At this point Plautius sent across Flavius Vespasianus (the future Emperor), and his elder brother Sabinus, who was acting as his lieutenant.[16] This force also succeeded in crossing the river, and killing many of the barbarians, who were not expecting them. The rest of the British forces however did not retreat, but on the next day joined issue with them again. There was an indecisive struggle, but at last Gnaeus Hosidius Geta (after being almost taken prisoner) managed to defeat them. For this achievement he was later awarded the *ornamenta triumphalia,* though he had never been consul. Then the Britons retired. . . .

Embodied in this unsatisfactory account are some of the elements of a great battle, lasting two days, which settled the fate of Britain for the next four centuries.

The best attempt to make sense of it is that of Mr A. R. Burn,[17] and we accept and follow his main points, though suggesting a different site for the battle. Dio's account appears to describe two separate crossings of the river. In the first the Gallic *auxilia* make a diversion by swimming over and attacking the British horses. The presence of chariots at this point suggests that the bank was held by tribal chieftains. The main purpose of this attack seems to have been to distract the attention of the Britons from the second crossing, which was made by the legionaries. The comment of Dio that they were not expected implies that this later crossing was made at another point, and that the army had carried out an outflanking operation, probably upstream, while the Britons were dealing with what they may have thought the main attack.

The legion chosen for this was the IInd *Augusta* under its commander Vespasian. Having secured a foothold on the opposite bank, his next step was probably to bring up a pontoon bridge or ferry boats to build up strength. The need for equipment to force a river and establish rapid access to the bridge-head would have been considered in the initial planning of the campaign, though the Thames may then have been in mind. The heavy train brought up in the rear of the advancing army would have included many kinds of equipment, mainly for siege work.

These operations occupied the first day. The Britons soon realised that the main threat came from the new bridge-head and that, unless they were able to wipe it out rapidly and completely, its strength would grow until they would have to deal with the main force of the army on the west bank of the river. Meanwhile, perhaps through the night, fresh legionaries had been poured into the bridge-head. There was now more than one legion, and a task force commander, Hosidius Geta, presumably the senior legionary *legatus*,[18] took over. Now came the critical stage. In the daylight hours of the second day the Britons gathered their full strength and flung themselves into the assault. They managed to drive a deep wedge into the Roman ranks and almost succeeded in splitting their opponents. Geta was nearly captured, and he would have been stationed in a central or even rearward position at Staff H.Q. But as more and fresh troops were poured across the Medway into the bridge-head the balance of strength changed. The Britons had spent themselves, and the Roman Army was ready to break out of its confined space into open order. The Britons retired, the Roman Army was left in full possession. The Battle of Britain of A.D. 43 was over. Although it was not fully appreciated at the time, the fate of Britain had been sealed.

It is difficult to believe that such a violent clash would not have left some permanent mark on the landscape. The Roman Army must have built temporary camps for their forces of the usual geometric pattern. So far nothing has been observed either from the air or on the ground resembling these features. Of the great battle there is only one archaeological trace, and that found as recently as 1958. This consists of a hoard of thirty-four gold coins found in the village of Bredgar[19] on the North Downs. The latest of these coins are four of Claudius struck during A.D. 41 and 42. This modest hoard may well represent part of the savings of a soldier or a centurion, buried for safety before the engagement and never reclaimed. The find spot, nine miles from Aylesford, lies on the Downs just before the descent towards the Medway; it may have been the site of one of the camps where the assault troops rested before the battle.

The course of the river battle, thus reconstructed from the scrappy notes of Dio, has a very modern ring. There is a swift crossing at an unexpected point to secure a foothold, however precarious, until armour can be pushed across. If the bridge-head can be pinched out at this stage before the real fighting strength is there, the venture fails. But Roman discipline and toughness just managed to hold the bridge-head until the tables could be turned. It was no easy victory, but a long and bitter struggle against an heroic and determined foe, ably led. But the Romans were unable to follow up rapidly as their cavalry *auxilia* were on the other bank. By the time they were brought across and set off in pursuit the Britons had executed a speedy withdrawal.

Dio continues:

> Thence the Britons fell back to the River Thames at a point near where it enters the sea and forms a large pool at high tide. Knowing the firm ground and the fords with much precision, they crossed the river without difficulty; but the Romans were not so successful. However, the Celts swam across again and some others got over by a bridge a little way upstream, after which they assailed the barbarians from several sides at once and cut down many of them. In pursuing the remainder incautiously, they got into swamps from which it was difficult to make their way out and so lost a number of men.

The situation seems clear enough. The British command managed to break off the engagement, withdraw the bulk of their men, and make an excape across the Thames into the Essex marshes. There are several low-lying places like the Erith Marshes along the Thames which might in those days have been flooded at high tide. Woe betide anyone venturing into these areas without any knowledge of the firm paths! The main problem in Dio's account is the mention of a bridge further upstream, which appears to have been left intact and unguarded. It would seem strange tactics for such a resourceful leader as Caratacus to have left the main route to Camulodunum so unguarded. Did he give in so easily or were there other factors not mentioned? There seems no doubt that the most difficult task facing the Roman Army was that of crossing the Thames, a very different proposition from the Medway. Plautius would have known some of the difficulties from a study of Caesar: how the river was only just fordable in one place and how the Britons had, in 54 B.C., protected the opposite bank by a fence of sharp stakes which continued below water level. Plautius may have known about the bridge from the traders who had probably already established a depôt nearby. Had the Romans managed to capture the bridge by surprise tactics? This brings us back to the possibility of a landing at Chichester. It would not have been impossible for the Atrebates, with Roman cavalry support, to make their way by forest paths across the heavy Wealden clays, and swoop suddenly down on the small British force detailed to hold the bridge. Did the British forces turn to cross the Thames into Essex because the pursuit was too hot, or had they heard that the bridge had fallen?

The heavy Medway defeat, followed so quickly by the loss of the bridge, showed all too clearly the strength and organisation of the Roman Army and must have thrown out all the plans of Caratacus. By now there would be news of the other British tribes. Some were already won over: now, as the conquerors showed their teeth, more would flock to the Roman side. His resources were now more slender, though his tribesmen and bodyguards would remain faithful. Where could he hope to hold the Romans, already probing into Essex? There was no line of natural defence between the Thames and the Belgic capital at Camulodunum. Should he die trapped behind the massive earthworks of the Colne peninsula? As he brooded over this problem more unpleasant news reached him. His brother Togodumnus had perished, presumably in some skirmish north of the Thames, or by treachery. The two brothers may not have been very close, but they were united in their hatred of Rome, and above all it was Togodumnus who could command the allegiance of the main part of the Belgic Kingdom. Perhaps some of the Belgic nobles began to waver, especially those of Verulamium.

Whatever dark thoughts Caratacus may have harboured, he must have realised that there was no hope of holding up the Roman advance towards the Belgic capital, and that once there the end would come swiftly. He was not alone in these forebodings. One of the great powers in Britain was the Druids. So much imaginative nonsense has been written about these priests and their cult that they are often dismissed by serious historians as unworthy of discussion. Their real power lay not so much in their secret rites, as in their control over the Celtic tribal aristocracy. It was the Druids who were responsible for the education of the children of the kings and notables. Their high priests were drawn from these ranks, and so accepted by the kings as advisers in matters political as well as religious. Nor were the Druids the special preserve of a particular tribe. They claimed universal support from all the Celtic peoples, not only in Britain but in Gaul as well. They were thus a strong unifying force in the Celtic world, as Caesar had found in Gaul. All their resources were now bent on holding back the influence of Rome. Druidism because of its strong anti-Roman political feeling could not survive in a Roman province. The Roman government, accepting any form of religion which did not meddle in politics, was prepared to stamp out Druidism with complete ruthlessness. Another example of this attitude is seen in the Jewish Wars later in the first century. Judaism had pitted itself against Rome, and the headquarters of the national religion, the Great Temple in Jerusalem, was destroyed with a savage thoroughness. The Druids in Britain would never compromise, and to them the *pax Romana* was anathema. To survive at all resistance must be continued, and Caratacus was their best instrument. They clearly saw the only hope of success in a withdrawal as far west as the Welsh mountains. Here was terrain which could be defended, and in it lived a tough hill-folk with courage and tenacity far exceeding that of the farmers of Essex. Caratacus, no doubt, saw this, but he had no standing in Wales. Now the headquarters of the Druids were in Mona (Anglesey), and the recent and famous find of treasure, the remains of a ritual deposit, from Llyn Cerrig Bach[20] attest their influence over the tribes of Britain. Theirs would have been the influence which commended Caratacus to the tribes of Wales, and secured his election as war-leader.

But, if Caratacus went to Wales, other leaders maintained a spirit of defiance among the Belgae. Dio relates:

> Shortly afterwards Togodumnus perished, but the Britons, so far from yielding, united all the more firmly to avenge his death. Because of this fact and because of the difficulties he had encountered at the Thames, Plautius became afraid, and instead of advancing any further, proceeded to guard what he had already won, and sent for Claudius. For he had been instructed to do this in case he met with any

particularly stubborn resistance and, in fact, extensive equipment including elephants had already been got together for the expedition.

This curious and paradoxical passage seems to contain garbled pieces of an official report, that of the commander to his emperor. Plautius found himself in a dilemma. He, had, thanks to the prowess of his army and good staff-work, subdued the main opposition in the lowlands of Britain. The way to the capital, Camulodunum, was open, and he must have soon realised that any further resistance once the Thames was crossed could hardly be serious. If he was not careful Plautius might find himself actually on the point of entering Camulodunum. This would have exceeded his instructions, as Dio makes apparent. Only the Imperator himself should lead his victorious troops into the enemy capital. A carefully worded dispatch must therefore be sent to Claudius, outlining all the difficulties to be overcome, and how the legate now found himself unable to proceed further without the leadership of the emperor in person. Dio gives us part of the official explanation: but one can easily read between the lines.

IV

Claudius received the dispatch in Rome and set off on the long journey by sea, road, and river to join the legions waiting for him by the Thames. About the composition of the force he took to Britain, and indeed the route followed, our sources are tantalisingly incomplete. A detachment of the Praetorian Guard, under their commander Rufrius Pollio, must have accompanied the emperor in the field. To do so was their duty, but here there is something more. The Praetorians, two years earlier, had placed Claudius on the throne; now they were to see him win the military glory expected from a prince of the line of Drusus and Germanicus. And then there were the elephants, whose presence is attested by Dio. They are more likely to have been for ceremonial than military purposes: the 'elephant corps' of Collingwood seems wide of the mark.[21] What one would like to know is whether Claudius brought reinforcements for the legions and auxiliaries already in Britain. If so, the obvious source of supply was from the Rhine armies: this consideration has a bearing on his possible route. Unfortunately none of the ancient authorities has anything to say on this point. Their attention is concentrated on the many distinguished senators who were invited to follow in Claudius' retinue as *comites Caesaris*. To receive such an invitation was not necessarily a mark of honour, for the company included, besides men whom the emperor delighted to honour, others whom he was afraid to leave behind. To this latter group belonged that ambitious and enigmatic figure, the Gallic senator Valerius Asiaticus. He had been a candidate for emperor at the death of Gaius: Claudius was later to encompass his death and revile his memory. Then there was Marcus Crassus Frugi, married to a descendant of Pompey, 'a man silly enough to be a possible emperor', in Seneca's trenchant phrase. For the moment Claudius was bent on conciliating this illustrious house; Crassus' son, Cn. Pompeius Magnus, had married Claudius' daughter Antonia, and was also included in Claudius' retinue. (The father was executed in A.D. 46, the son too came to a bad and unedifying end.) Others were M. Vinicius (consul in A.D. 30 and again in 45), the husband of Claudius' niece Julia, and perhaps Sentius Saturninus, whose equivocal role at the time of the assassination of Gaius we have already noted. Junius Silanus, betrothed to the infant Octavia, belonged to what has been called 'the family party', as did Plautius Silvanus Aelianus, related both to the emperor and to Aulus Plautius. On Claudius' personal staff were his doctor, Xenophon, and the eunuch and freedman Posides, who presumably served as secretary in charge of the imperial correspondence.

For the progress of the invasion of Britain, the most important of these *comites Caesaris* was the future emperor, Servius Sulpicius Galba. Rich and powerful, a connection of the Empress Livia, he was now aged forty-six, and had become the trusted adviser of Claudius. As Governor of Upper Germany under Gaius and Claudius he had been outstandingly successful, crushing German attacks on Gaul in A.D. 40, and winning a victory over the warlike Chatti in 41. These successes were due to his qualities as a disciplinarian as well as commander in the field: he devised stiff programmes of training for the recruits to his army, and set an example of personal fitness and devotion to duty. As the man with the most recent experience of warfare in northern Europe, he would be well qualified to act as Claudius' adviser in his British command, and to make an independent assessment of the military situation. Suetonius, our sole authority for Galba's presence in Britain, refers to it in an oblique manner which had given rise to misunderstanding: '. . . so high was his standing with Claudius, that, when he was afflicted by a sudden but by no means dangerous illness, the date of the British expedition was postponed'.[22] How is this to be taken? A postponement of the whole project from an earlier year to A.D. 43 ? A postponement of the sailing of the force under Aulus Plautius? Better than either, we suggest, a postponement of the sailing of Claudius' own '*expeditio*' from Boulogne: reasons of time and space alike make this the best context for Galba's sudden but not dangerous illness.

The route followed by the imperial expedition reflects Claudius' interest in water transport. From Rome it proceeded down the Tiber to Ostia, soon to be the scene of a magnificent scheme of harbour improvement. The next stage, by sea to Massilia, was a most uncomfortable one, due to severe gales. Suetonius[23] records that the emperor was twice nearly shipwrecked—once off the Ligurian coast and again off the Iles d'Hyères. The reader is always left to sift for himself the serious from the trivial in Suetonius. This is more than gossip. Suetonius is at pains to emphasise that the storms were caused by the '*circius*'—the swirling wind, that dry, cold, catabatic wind known in Provence as the mistral, so harrying to the nerves of the inhabitants of Rhône Valley, and destructive of shipping in the Gulf of Lyons. It was famous in antiquity, and Augustus built it a temple, on the basis of what experiences we do know. But if Claudius' encounters with the mistral had resulted in the loss of that distinguished passenger-list, how different Roman history would have been! No Nero, no Year of the Four Emperors. . . . But in fact Marseilles was safely reached, and they began the journey across Gaul. If Marseilles was the port of entry, Boulogne was certainly the port of exit. But what was the route followed? Authorities differ: Suetonius says that Claudius marched north to Boulogne; Dio that he went 'partly by land and partly by river to the Ocean . . .'. There need not be a contradiction: in any case, the more specific statement of Dio is perhaps to be preferred. And, if so, which rivers were used? A glance at the map would suggest the Rhône from Marseilles to Lyons and thence by the Saône—but to travel against the current of the Rhône does not make for speed. Besides, Dio's words strongly suggest that the rivers in question flowed into the Channel or the North Sea. The Rhine is the most likely of these northern rivers, and one begins to think of the great road, built by Claudius, from Andematunnum in Central Gaul to Bonna (Bonn) on the Rhine. Embarkation would be possible at Bonn itself, or even at Trier on the Moselle: near the mouth of the Rhine use could be made of Drusus' canal for a quick connection to the North Sea. More circuitous than the direct overland route to Boulogne, such a journey would enable Claudius to show himself to the armies along the Rhine, and to pick up reinforcements as he went. Or they might have been brought by Galba to some such rendezvous as Bonn, Neuss, or Cologne. But these arguments are inconclusive, and must not be pressed. Whatever route was followed, the port of embarkation for Britain was Boulogne.

'The Channel crossing was uneventful.' The words are those of Suetonius, and one may fairly read into them the wholly understandable relief of those who made the voyage. If the Roman sea (*mare nostrum*) had treated Claudius with such disrespect, what might not be expected of Oceanus himself? But no: this, the eighth crossing of the English Channel by a Roman armada, was the smoothest to date. We are nowhere told where they landed in Britain, and this has led to conjecture. But surely the only possible place is Rutupiae, where anchorage, supplies, and barracks for the troops were all in a state of readiness? Here, we may be confident, the soil of Britain was for the first time trodden by a Roman Emperor.

It would be gratifying if we could give a date for this historic occasion with even the degree of accuracy possible in the case of Caesar's first expedition. In 55 B.C., Caesar anchored off Dover about 9.00 on a day in late August—probably the 26th. For Claudius a much greater margin of error must be allowed. Aulus Plautius' message—whether sent by some signal system or by courier we do not know—could have taken up to a week to reach Rome. The storms in the Mediterranean suggest at least a week for the voyage from Ostia to Marseilles: anything from three weeks to a month must then be allowed for the imperial party to cross Gaul. In short, if we suppose that Plautius sent his message in the first half of August, the imperial presence cannot have graced Britain much before mid-September. Very little of the campaigning season was left, and there would be anxiety to get back to the Continent before the 'equinoctial gales' whose existence was so firmly credited. Here lies the explanation for Claudius' short stay of only sixteen days in Britain.

It is tempting to ask what use Aulus Plautius made of August and early September, and hard to believe that he spent it, as Dio says, 'guarding what he had won'. Two possibilities suggest themselves, on indirect evidence. The fact that Verulamium was given municipal status by the Romans and that it was an object of especial hatred to Boudicca's rebels, suggests that, about this time, a section of the Catuvellauni went over to the Romans. Was this the fruit of negotiations in which, perhaps, Adminius may have had a hand? The second arises from Suetonius' statement that the victories of Vespasian's campaign in the south-west were gained 'partly under the command of Aulus Plautius, partly under that of Claudius'.[24] Now if Claudius was in Britain for sixteen days only and Vespasian's expedition was already under way, it follows that the arrangements for mounting it must have been undertaken by Aulus Plautius during this period of waiting for the Emperor. If these suggestions are accepted, it would seem that he did not waste his time. Only in two sectors were the enemy still in the field—on the approaches to Camulodunum, and in the lands of the Durotriges and the western Belgae. The second was now the major threat, and Vespasian would have it in hand. The forces defending Camulodunum could be relied upon to provide enough—but not too much—opposition for the imperial commander-in-chief.

Dio is the authority for the statement that Claudius took over the command from Aulus Plautius on the Thames. For the events that followed there is a direct conflict of evidence between him and Suetonius. Dio, as will be seen from Appendix I, speaks of a river crossing, a victorious battle against the Britons beyond the Thames, the capture of Camulodunum, and possibly a further period of fighting, resulting in the surrender of 'many British tribes'. Suetonius is emphatic that 'no battle or bloodshed' preceded the surrender of 'a portion of the island'. At first sight the statement of Josephus seems to reinforce Suetonius, for he says that Vespasian had 'by his military genius added Britain, a land previously unknown, to the Empire, thus affording Claudius . . . a triumph without any exertion on his own part'. But Josephus' purpose is to flatter Vespasian at all costs: not only does he disparage Claudius, but omits any reference to Aulus Plautius and to the Medway battle. Moreover Suetonius himself says that a pageant of the sacking of Camulodunum was later enacted on the Campus Martius, which makes it clear that some British resistance must have been encountered.[25] We have no means of knowing how serious it was, nor under whose leadership. Togodumnus was dead; Caratacus, presumably, already in the west. The sixteen days spent by Claudius in Britain obviously leave no time for a campaign, but there is no need to reject Dio's statement that actions were fought in which Claudius received from his troops the tribute of being hailed as 'Imperator'. And if they departed from established form in so hailing him 'more than once in the same war', it was by no means the only such departure in that remarkable reign.

There can be little doubt that the ceremonies to be staged in the enemy capital were the real objective of the imperial presence. No description survives, but it is clear from the inscription on the Arch of Claudius and from Dio that they must have taken place. They are to be compared with the 'Durbars', as they have been called, held on more than one occasion by Julius Caesar in Gaul. Their object would be to overawe the British kings and notables by a display of Roman majesty, and to instruct them in the obligations they would have to meet once the province of Britannia was established. We can assume that they were carefully planned. The elephants—a thoughtful touch —were there for the triumphal entry into Camulodunum. Whatever the demeanour of Claudius himself (and his *bêtises* on formal state occasions were notorious and mercilessly recorded), they at least would lend dignity to the occasion.

But the most impressive ceremony must have been the formal surrender of the British kings, in the presence of the Emperor and his retinue, the Praetorian Guard, Aulus Plautius, and high officers

THE INVASION AND THE DEFEAT OF THE BELGIC KINGDOM

of the invading force. This must have been a spectacle to efface memories of the court of 'the radiant Cymbeline'. According to the inscriptions on the arches at Rome and Cyzicus, eleven British kings 'formally placed themselves under the sway of the Roman people' (see Appendix III). Claudius later received a free hand from the Senate to conclude such agreements as he thought necessary in Britain, and here he effectively gathered the fruits of both war and diplomacy. We can identify some, but not all, of the British eleven. An attempt to do so in some detail is made in Appendix III (p. 185). Certainly they will have included the rulers of the three client-kingdoms now set up among the Brigantes, the Iceni and the Regnenses. Their formal act of homage completed the first phase of the invasion. The Belgic power was shattered and the groundwork of the Roman province laid. But the next phase was to prove slower, more costly and more difficult than may have been foreseen in the plan.

A special session of the Senate was held immediately the news of Claudius' British victories was announced in Rome by his messengers, Cn. Pompeius Magnus and Lucius Junius Silanus. They were chosen for this mission as the sons-in-law of Claudius, and so the most suitable representatives of the imperial house. There is piquancy in the fact that the descendant of Pompey the Great, recently permitted to renew that famous name, should announce to the Senate that the work of Julius Caesar in Britain had been fulfilled—or should one say excelled? It will have appealed to Claudius, who combined *pietas* and a feeling for history with a highly individual sense of humour. Nor will it have been lost on the Senate. The honours which were then accorded to Claudius, his wife, and his son had presumably been decided in advance. For Claudius, a triumph and the erection of two triumphal arches, one in Rome and the other on the Channel coast—perhaps on the precedent of the three arches granted to the younger Drusus in A.D. 23 in Rome, on the banks of the Rhine and on Mt Amanus in Syria. For Claudius and his son, the title of Britannicus: in the same way, the title of Germanicus had been conferred on the elder Drusus and his male descendants. For Messalina, the seat of dignity that Livia had been granted, and the privilege of using the *carpentum*, the two-wheeled car used by Vestal

Virgins and high officials on state occasions. Thus early in the reign appear those tendencies which, as Charlesworth has said, transformed the household of Claudius into something like a royal family.[26]

The triumph itself was held in 44, on a most lavish scale.[27] It was, after all, the first celebrated by a reigning *Princeps* since the triple triumph of Augustus in 29 B.C.—more than seventy years earlier. As an exceptional measure, the governors of provinces were permitted to leave their posts and come to Rome for the occasion. So, too, were certain exiles, but we are not told whether this exercise of the Imperial *clementia* went as far as a full amnesty. Suetonius and Dio comment on some of the more remarkable features of the ceremony. Claudius himself gave an exemplary display of old-fashioned *pietas* when he ascended the steps of the Capitoline temple on his knees—as Julius Caesar had done—supported by his sons-in-law. Messalina in her *carpentum* followed the triumphal chariot. Behind, on foot (following the precedent established by Augustus), came the commanders on whom the *triumphalia ornamenta* were to be conferred. They included the future Emperor Vespasian, fresh from his successful campaigns in south-west Britain, and Gn. Hosidius Geta, who had done good service at the Medway battle. M. Crassus Frugi, receiving *triumphalia ornamenta* for the second time, was allowed the privilege of riding on horseback. Among others who had served in Britain were the future Emperor Galba—whose illness had caused Claudius to postpone his departure from Rome—and Vespasian's elder brother Flavius Sabinus. The comment that Claudius was unusually lavish in distributing honours seems unwarranted on this occasion. Literary sources, papyri, and inscriptions add a few other details to what is known of the triumph. *Aurum coronarium*, the gold wreaths sent by cities and provinces, was clearly on a lavish scale. Pliny singles out those from Gaul and Spain, but unfortunately the text is doubtful where he gives the figures for their weight. Other wreaths were contributed by guilds and corporations, and we have the text of the letter of acknowledgement sent by Claudius to the Guild of Travelling Athletes. An inscription from Pisidian Antioch records the decorations bestowed on P. Anicius Maximus, *praefectus castrorum* of the IInd Legion *ob bellum Britannicum*, presumably on this

13　*A triumphal arch commemorating Claudius' victory over the Britons —'DE BRITTAN [IS]'— and showing the Emperor mounted between piles of trophies*

From an aureus of Claudius

14　*Claudius in triumph after his British campaign*

From a cameo

15 *A column of the Praetorian Guard on the march*
From Trajan's Column

occasion.[28] One should also take note of a group of eight poems in the Latin Anthology, all of which commemorate the Claudian invasion, and were presumably written for the triumph.[29] As *vers d'occasion*, they have a value of their own, for the business of a poet laureate, actual or would-be, is to say the obvious and say it well. We may expect them, then, to stress those features of the Claudian invasion which attracted most public comment, and in the way the government desired—to versify the headlines, as it were. What those features were is best seen in number 426—a poem of quality, which ought to be better known:

> *Semota et vasto disiuncta Britannia ponto,*
> *cinctaque inaccessis horrida litoribus,*
> *quam pater invictis Nereus velaverat undis,*
> *quam fallax aestu circuit Oceanus,*
> *brumalem sortita polum, qua frigida semper*
> *praefulget stellis Arctos inocciduis,*
> *conspectu devicta tuo, Germanice Caesar,*
> *subdidit insueto colla premenda iugo.*
> *aspice, confundat populos ut pervia tellus;*
> *coniunctum est, quod adhuc orbis et orbis erat.*

The poet speaks first of Britain herself: her remoteness 'set apart in the boundless ocean'; her inaccessible shores (an echo, this, of Julius Caesar's experiences, though Claudius had found a good harbour at Richborough); the treacherous tides (another echo of Julius Caesar); the wintry climate, and the chilly, never-setting Bear that rules the British skies. Then the speed of the Claudian conquest: 'she surrendered as soon as she saw you, Caesar'—for Claudius was only in Britain for sixteen days. Finally, the reflection that there are no barriers left, and that what were once two separate worlds are joined into one. 'The world is small', said Christopher Columbus; the conquest of Britain seems to have produced in the Roman world the same feeling of barriers down. The other poems do not add much to the repertory of themes. From a reading of the poems as a whole, three leading motifs emerge, the conquest of the Ocean, the lightning campaign of Claudius, and the enlarged horizons now that the remote, mysterious island is brought into the Roman world.

Before looking at the inscription from the Arch of Claudius, together with what else is known of that monument, it is worth considering, in its completed form, the grand design for the architectural commemoration of Claudius' British victories.[30] It begins on the Palatine, where on the gable of the Imperial Palace were placed the spoils won from the enemy, the civic crown, and next to it, the naval crown 'the sign of the crossing and, as it were, the conquest of Ocean'. This was done immediately after the return of Claudius to Rome in the autumn of 43. But the main monument, the Arch of Claudius in Rome, was not dedicated until 52. Its site was carefully chosen. Standing in the Via Lata, it bridged the great artery (now the Corso) leading from the Forum and Capitol to the Porta Flaminia and the road to the north, to Gaul and to Britain itself. It was also a clever choice in terms of the topography of Rome. For this part of the Campus Martius had been developed by Augustus and was dominated by great buildings and monuments associated with him. A little further along the Via Lata was the Ara Pacis, further still, the Mausoleum of Augustus. The Arch of Claudius itself carried a branch of the Aqua Virgo (restored by Claudius after the neglect of Gaius) to the Pantheon and the Thermae of Agrippa, the work of Augustus' great minister. Thus the siting of the Arch of Claudius proclaimed his British conquests Urbi et Orbi, and brought him into association with Augustus. On the shores of the Channel, reached by a network of roads of Claudian construction, stood another triumphal arch dedicated by the Senate 'at the point whence he had set sail'. There can be no doubt that this was Gesoriacum (Boulogne), whose harbour Claudius had enlarged to make it the most important port on the North Sea. The date of the dedication of this arch is unknown and nothing of it survives. But it is not fanciful to suppose that it was built, not simply to commemorate Claudius' departure from the mainland, but as a deliberate counter to the equivocal monument of Gaius, at once lighthouse and 'trophy'. Claudius had done more than gather shells. The arch at Gesoriacum commemorated an authentic victory, and in the traditional Roman manner. Finally, there was the Temple of Claudius at Camulodunum, the royal seat of Cunobelinus and the capital of the regnum Britanniae; the scene, too, of the surrender of the British kings. It was intended to mark the permanence of Roman rule in Britain; Boudicca and her followers were right in regarding it as 'the citadel of eternal slavery'.

It has been shown that the four honorific inscriptions to members of the Imperial House imply that the arch of Claudius is to be compared to the Arch of Augustus at Pavia, with its inscriptions to eight (or nine?) members of the Julian House.[31] Moreover, the representation on the coinage issued in A.D. 46, 49, 50 and 51, of an arch crowned by an equestrian statue between two trophies may well refer to this arch (*13*). Though the conquering rider is absent from Roman art of the first century A.D., except for the Arch of Drusus, it accords well enough with Claudius' *pietas* that he should have taken that arch as a model. A large part of the dedicatory inscription is preserved in the courtyard of the Conservatori Museum in Rome (*44*). Its interpretation raises several problems, which are discussed in Appendix III (p. 185).

Aulus Plautius
and the Shaping
of a British Province

A.D. 43–47

4

On his departure from Britain, says Dio, Claudius 'deprived the conquered of their arms and handed them over to Plautius, bidding him also to subjugate the remaining districts'. Which were the remaining districts, and what exactly was the task assigned to Aulus Plautius? Tacitus' remark that 'the nearer part of Britain was gradually reduced into the shape of a Roman province'[1] is of some help, though strictly speaking it covers the governorship of Aulus Plautius and that of his successor Ostorius Scapula. Plautius' share in this programme can be deduced from what he is known to have accomplished. When he left Britain in A.D. 47 the recalcitrant tribes of the south-west had been reduced by Vespasian, and a *limes* had been established which ran from the Bristol Channel by way of the lower reaches of the Severn, the Warwickshire Avon, and the Trent, to the Humber. In political terms this made a province out of the old empire of Cunobelinus, with most of the territory of the Dobunni, Durotriges and Coritani. A modern geographer would see it as the subjugation of the lowlands of Britain as far as the western edge of the limestone belt that stretches from Mendip to the Lincoln Wolds. In terms of contemporary social and economic planning, we may see in it an early version of the plan for the south-east. The military phase of this operation was a triple advance into the interior of the island: first, Vespasian's campaigns in the south-west, ending probably at Exeter: second, along the line of Watling Street into the midlands, perhaps to High Cross: the third, northwards to Lincoln and the Humber. Once these objectives were obtained, a network of strategic roads and forts had to be constructed. In the midlands, where potentially hostile peoples lay beyond the Severn and Trent, this took the form of a defensive zone which is implied in the construction of a Roman *limes*. Vespasian's campaign in the south-west was probably completed by the end of the campaigning season of A.D. 43, since he was in Rome to receive his honours at the triumph of A.D. 44. No timetable can be given for the other two campaigns, nor indeed is it known whether any fighting was involved. Very probably the Roman troops, as so often, were employed as engineers rather than as combatant soldiers. Their training fitted them equally well for such tasks, and from Trajan's Column we can see how much of the time of troops in the field was devoted to the cutting of wood and turf, the siting and construction of forts and signal-stations, the gathering and transport of food and supplies[11, 36].

II

We begin, then, with the drive to the south-west. It has been suggested above that it was probably launched before Claudius' arrival in Britain: also, that it was a land–sea campaign, starting perhaps from Chichester harbour. The historical evidence comes from the life of Vespasian by Suetonius Tranquillus, in which he says: 'On the accession of Claudius, Vespasian was indebted to Narcissus for the command of a legion in Germany: and proceeded to Britain where he fought thirty battles, subjugated two warlike tribes and captured more than twenty *oppida*, besides the Isle of Wight.'[2] This places the commander and his legion, the IInd *Augusta*, firmly in the south-west and committed to a serious campaign. It is doubtful whether the other parts of England being occupied at that time would have offered so great a resistance, and it seems to have been hardly by chance that Vespasian was chosen by Plautius for the toughest assignment. He has shown his ability in the Medway battle and rewarded Plautius for the confidence placed in him. While most of the British tribes had by this time capitulated—either by Roman persuasion in advance or by their own recognition of the superiority of Roman arms—it is clear from archaeological evidence that the Durotriges of Dorset and Somerset remained implacably hostile and that their strongholds had to be taken by storm one by one.

The second conquered tribe must be either the Belgae or the Dumnonii (as they were later called), to the north and the west of the Durotriges respectively. There is as yet little direct evidence to

16   *Maiden Castle in Dorset, a British Iron Age hill-fort, which was stormed and sacked by Vespasian's legion*

17 *A Roman catapult-bolt lodged in the backbone of a Durotrigian warrior*
Part of a skeleton found in the war cemetery at Maiden Castle

18 *A carro-ballista, a spring gun (which would have shot a bolt*
similar to that shown above) mounted on a cart
From Trajan's Column

decide between them.[3] The excavations in 1934-5 at Hembury, a hill-fort just in the Dumnonian area, produced Roman pottery of Claudian date and a Claudian coin, and it was shown that at a late date in the fort's history part of the defences was destroyed by fire and the ramparts slighted.[4] At Worlebury, a hill-fort in Somerset overlooking the Bristol Channel, eighteen skeletons were found with signs of battle wounds, also there was evidence of destruction and slighting, and early Roman coins,[5] but the evidence is as yet insufficient for any conclusions to be drawn. Mention might here be made of the remarkable hoard of horse-gear brought up by the plough at Polden Hill, near Bridgwater in Somerset, in 1800.[6] This barbaric array, its glittering enamels dulled by decay, suggests a wealthy British horseman, though it could also have come from a Roman cavalryman of a Celtic auxiliary unit.

The term 'Belgae' may have been a convenient one for the Roman authorities when marking out the boundaries of the tribes in the establishment of provincial government. This would probably have meant the grouping together of a number of small tribes with a common ethnic background whose names have been lost. The earliest coinage of this area has been shown to be derived from the Atrebates[7] to the east, and the suggestion is made that this was due to a westward movement of a section of the Atrebates loyal to the memory of their dynastic head Commius, who fled from Caesar vowing he would never look a Roman in the face again. This tribal movement must have taken place after the skilful diplomacy of Augustus had won them over to form the main pro-Roman element in Britain. Those who rejected this change of loyalty joined the western branch which may have already spread in this direction.[8] If there is any substance in this interesting theory it would imply that anti-Roman feeling might have led to active hostility in concert with the Durotriges. On balance one would favour the western Atrebates, rather than the Dumnonii, as the second warlike tribe.

About the attitude of the Durotriges there can be no doubt. Their great fortress of Maiden Castle near Dorchester was the scene of a large-scale excavation in 1934-7 by Sir Mortimer Wheeler.[9] The investigation of this most imposing of all British hill-forts produced important conclusions about the people who lived there. It was suggested by Wheeler that the multiplicity of ditches and ramparts was due to the introduction of sling-warfare into Britain, and he looked to the source of this in the defeat of the Veneti of Brittany by Julius Caesar in 56 B.C. Some of these tribesmen, he suggested, fled to Britain and established themselves in Dorset. Wheeler never regarded his work at Maiden Castle as completed, and it was unfortunate that the last war prevented any further steps to bring this suggested chronology and its implications to a satisfactory conclusion. Nevertheless a further important stage was reached with the publication of the *Hill-forts of Northern France* in 1957,[10] the result of excavation and field-work intended to establish the cultural connection between Brittany and Dorset. It is evident that these explorations, while illuminating the problems of the Iron Age in north-western Gaul, in fact failed to produce the necessary links. Even so, it has only been in recent years that Wheeler's views have been seriously challenged,[11] and current opinion is that the history of the Durotriges is longer and more complicated than originally supposed.

The origins and level of prehistoric cultures can often be judged by their pottery and metalwork. Durotrigian pottery has distinctive characteristics[12] but appears to be derived from several different sources. At the time of the Roman conquest, many of the Early Iron Age forms still persisted. But the wheel had been introduced, and a group of the latest native pottery at Maiden Castle consisted of fine bead-rim bowls with an almost lustrous surface, suggesting that the potters may have been imitating metalwork. Belgic influence is marginal, and there is nothing to suggest that the Durotriges had been Belgicised to the same degree as the Dobunni. Some indication of the extent of Durotrigian territory can be gained from the distribution of their pottery types, which matches quite well the evidence of the coins. The coinage seems to have originally derived from a Gallic type brought into Britain along the south coast by settlers early in the first century B.C.; later it developed into distinctive local forms.[13] Unfortunately none of the Durotrigian coins are inscribed with the possible exception of the two unusual examples bearing the enigmatic letters 'CRAB'.[14] While the precise function of such coins in the Celtic economy is not understood, it seems clear from the distribution of their find spots that they do not stray in large numbers from a well-defined area. This concentration[15] in the case of the Durotriges shows boundaries to the east on the River Avon, to the north the River Wylye, and to the west the River Axe, thus including the whole of Dorset with parts of Wiltshire and possibly Somerset and east Devon. The eastern frontier may even extend to the River Test which flows into Southampton Water. But the area between the Test and the Avon is the New Forest which has so far yielded little archaeological evidence of this period, and is hardly likely to do so in its present condition.

Of all the great hill-forts of Britain those of Wessex are the most impressive by their sheer size and complexity. They usually occupy a hill-top position, with the encircling ramparts and ditches cut along the contours. Excavations show that in many cases these sites have a long and complex history, often starting with a small fairly simple type of defence, such as a single ditch and bank reinforced with timber. Towards the end of the Iron Age much larger areas are enclosed, with several sets of ditches, and the entrances become almost labyrinthine. The ditches and banks, often cut on a steep slope, were formed by excavating the ditch and heaping the spoil on either or both lips, according to the nature of the ground. Where necessary the fronts were revetted in timber, stone, or a combination of both. Sometimes, as at Maiden Castle, the construction is of the *glacis* type, i.e. the slope of the ditch is continued up the bank without a break. On the south side of this great hill-fort there are four banks and three ditches spanning a horizontal distance of about 450 feet. Even today, in their slighted and weather-worn state, they present an impressive obstacle. But the most extraordinary features of these defences are the gateways. The entrances are so designed that all approaches to the final gap in the rampart are by an oblique, circuitous route overlooked the whole way by the cliff-like banks. The exact purpose of this remarkable defence in depth is not clear. At one time it was attributed simply to the introduction of the sling. As the attackers toiled up and down these obstacles they would be under attack from slingers from above who would have the advantage of height. The large piles of sling stones found on these hill-forts are evidence of this method of defence, but the explanation cannot be so simple. The bank and counterscarp normally create dead ground where attackers could lie and rest before the next rush; slingers stationed on the top of the innermost bank would only have them as targets for part of the time. There must have been some arrangement for defenders to occupy a more advanced position so that they could engage the enemy more closely—especially at the entrances—though to do so a means of easy retreat would have been needed. In this respect the native works differ from the Roman defences, where everything is controlled from the rampart top from which the entire ditch system is under direct line of fire.

These Iron Age defences may have been adequate in intertribal warfare. Against the organisation and equipment of the Roman Army they were of little avail. There is no evidence from any of the British hill-forts to suggest that they withstood direct assault for very long. If this had failed, the Army would have settled down to a siege and thrown round the whole fortress a great circumvallation, which would have left its traces. They would then have pressed forward a series of attacks with specially designed engines and battering rams. The Romans regarded themselves as supreme in this type of warfare. Julius Frontinus, an eminent general and a later Governor of Britain, in his Introduction to Book III of his *Stratagems*, stated rather complacently that 'the invention of engines of war [for siegecraft] has long since reached its limit and I see no further hope of improvements in the applied arts . . .'. What the Roman army could do when fully extended is vividly illustrated in the account of the siege of Jotapata in A.D. 67, as given by Josephus (*Bellum Judaicum*, III, 141–339). The passage deserves to be read as a whole: besides its merits as a military narrative, there is the added interest that it is written by the Jewish commander, and that his Roman opponent was none other than Vespasian, now, in Josephus' words, 'grown grey in the service of Rome'. Here only the briefest summary can be attempted. Jotapata, the modern Jefat, was a position of immense natural strength, since the town was surrounded by precipitous cliffs on three sides, and strongly fortified on the fourth. Vespasian surrounded it by a double line of infantry and an outer ring of cavalry. Next archers and slingers were used to clear away all Jewish resistance outside the walls: but repeated sallies by the defenders led to five days of indecisive fighting. Then the Romans constructed earthworks opposite the fortifications of the town: this completed, they brought up 160 pieces of artillery and opened fire on the defenders. 'Simultaneously, the catapults discharged their bolts, stones of 100-lb. weight were hurled by the stone-projectors, there was a hail of firebrands and of arrows. As a result, not merely were the Jews driven from the ramparts, but the whole area behind them was untenable if it came within range. . . .' But Jewish counter-attacks drove the Romans from their firing-position, while fatigue parties working day and night raised the height of the wall by sixty feet. Vespasian now settled down to a blockade, relying on lack of water to force the Jews to surrender. This did not happen without much further fighting, culminating in a Roman night assault combined with an appalling artillery bombardment. At last, after forty-seven days of siege, an attack delivered in the darkness before dawn and led by the future emperor Titus carried the citadel, and the town was lost. A general massacre followed. The total casualties in the siege are given as 40,000.

Operations on this scale were of course not called for in Britain: indeed, in their complexity of technique they exceed anything employed by Caesar in the war against Vercingetorix. It is unfortunate that no historian describes in detail the capture of a British hill-fort. Little help can be got from Caesar's account of the sieges of Gergovia and Alesia in Gaul, where vastly greater numbers were involved on both sides. The immensely strong natural position of Uxellodunum (Puy d'Issolu) was a last-ditch stand by 2,000 desperate men. It fell because the Romans succeeded in depriving the Gauls of access to water. It is unlikely that Vespasian ever needed this ultimate weapon. An account by Tacitus[16] of one of Germanicus' battles gives an idea of a method likely to have been used against the hill-forts of Wessex. The key position was a broad earthwork 'built by the Angrivarii to divide their lands from the Cherusci'. The German infantry were stationed on this earthwork. The Roman legionaries at first found it impossible to carry the position by assault, for, says Tacitus, 'scaling the earthwork was like trying to climb a wall, and the troops were seriously harassed from above. Germanicus saw that at close quarters the odds would be heavily against him, so the legions withdrew a short distance and two kinds of slingers were advanced to discharge

97

their missiles and dislodge the enemy. The artillery fired bolts: the more the defenders exposed themselves, the more readily they were wounded and brought down.' It was in fact, Roman control of artillery fire of various calibres that made it impossible to defend the Celtic hill-forts. The *catapultae* could direct heavy and continuous fire against key-points, such as gateways and defended entrances. Josephus gives some impression of the terrifying effects of a Roman bombardment. A heavy stone from a Roman engine knocked off the head of a Jewish soldier: it was found three furlongs away. The noise and crash of the missiles were interminable. The more mobile slingers could quickly break up smaller concentrations along the walls. By now the way would be clear for the legionaries to advance to a spot selected for assault. No doubt they often employed the famous *testudo* or 'tortoise' formation (*19*), where the legionaries locked shields over their heads. The *testudo* was not without its troubles against a fortified city. Thus at the siege of Cremona we find the defenders harassing the *testudo* with large stones and poles and even— a heart-warming moment surely—toppling down a *ballista* on to it. At Jotapata the defenders made good use of boiling oil—without, however, halting the Roman assault. But even if the Celtic warriors had had such resources they could not have stayed in position to use them. Superior fire-power had nullified the whole idea of the hill-fort, which was to render impregnable a single strong point. By now the only purpose they served was to collect the fighting strength of the tribes into a series of convenient receptacles, ready for a Roman force to pick them off. Vespasian's army seems to have regarded itself as a specialist in hill-fort operations; the result must have been a sort of competition to see how quickly it could be done. During the forty-seven days of the siege of Jotapata Vespasian may have thought nostalgically of the simpler problems of the hill-forts of Wessex.

We must now attempt to identify the twenty hill-forts taken by Vespasian. In only three or four cases is there archaeological evidence of hill-forts attacked by the Roman Army—Maiden Castle, Hod Hill, Spettisbury Rings and Ham Hill. In the first of these, the evidence took the gruesome but dramatic form of a small cemetery of warriors buried at the east gate. The twenty-eight graves had been hastily dug,

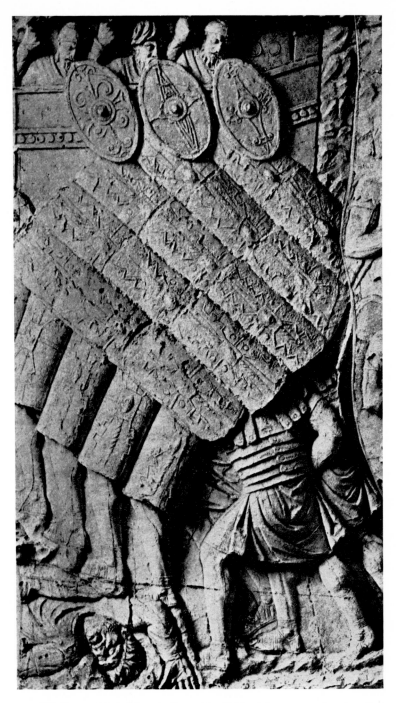

19   *The Roman 'testudo', a tactic used to shield mining or ramming operations*
From Trajan's Column

20–1   *Skulls of warriors, showing the fatal sword cuts*

22   *A Durotrigian warrior with his tankard*

FROM THE WAR CEMETERY AT MAIDEN CASTLE

and the bodies thrust in with joints of meat and mugs of liquid to sustain and refresh their souls on their long journey. Many of the bodies still bore, on skulls, spines, and other bones, evidence of the sword cuts which had dispatched them (*20–1*). There were twenty-three male and eleven female skeletons. Some of the extensive skull injuries are eloquent of the professional skill of the legionaries in delivering their forceful blows; though other evidence makes it quite apparent that the bodies were mutilated after death. The same soldiers were also capable of taking brutal but senseless revenge on their victims for the trouble given and losses incurred. The most striking of all this evidence comes from a body with the head of a Roman *ballista* bolt still fixed into the vertebrae (*17*). The bolt had entered the body high in the chest and travelled down and through the trunk, slicing a vertebra and coming to rest with its point projecting from the back. Maiden Castle produced details of how Roman soldiers had slighted the ramparts and gateways, pulling out and scattering massive limestone blocks to ensure that the army would not have to take this fortress again. Yet there are no signs round this imposing hill-fort of any Roman siege works. The assault must have been swift and decisive and it says much for the skill of the legionaries in attacking such a seemingly difficult position.

The other hill-fort to yield evidence of a Roman attack is Hod Hill near Stourpaine, about eighteen miles in a direct line north-east of Maiden Castle. This site has been excavated for the Trustees of the British Museum by Professor I. A. Richmond, whose main interest was the Roman fort built in one of the corners of the Iron Age fortress. During the course of this work it became necessary to examine the Iron Age hut-circles to see if the natives remained there during the Roman military occupation. Around one of the larger huts the excavators found a number of Roman *ballista* bolt-heads which had been aimed at this target, perhaps a rallying point round the chieftain after the tribesmen had been driven from the ramparts. There is evidence here also that the work of strengthening one of the gateways was never completed.[17]

The evidence from the third site is by no means as reliable but is nevertheless highly suggestive. It comes from the single-ditched hill-fort known as Spettisbury Rings, three miles south-east of Blandford.

In 1857 the Central Dorset Railway between Blandford and Wimborne was being constructed, and a deep cutting sliced off part of the defences of the hill-fort. What was described as a large pit[18] would seem more likely to have been part of the ditch, and in it were found eighty or ninety skeletons. Some of the skeletons showed signs of battle: one skull had a piece sliced away; another was found with a spear-head still embedded in it. Only part of the objects found with the burials were recovered: these are now in the British Museum. They include lance and spear-heads of Roman military types as well as fragments of bronze scabbard bindings and a length of shield binding. These finds indicate a mass burial of war victims, and the associated remains of Roman equipment point strongly to this as another example of the Roman Army at work. The difference between this and Maiden Castle is that in the latter the natives were able to give their kinsfolk a decent though hasty burial, while at Spettisbury there may have been a mass slaughter. There the Roman soldiers threw the bodies into the ditch and pushed the upper part of the rampart on top of them, as they did later at Sutton Walls in Herefordshire.[19]

At Ham Hill in Somerset, famous for its fine stone, excavations by St George Gray revealed a considerable quantity of Roman military equipment, including a large piece of a jerkin with bronze scales,[20] now in Taunton Museum. The site of this discovery clearly indicates the presence of a Roman Army unit on a small plateau adjacent to the 200-acre hill-fort. The relationship may be similar to that at Hod Hill. Only careful excavation will enable the list of hill-forts stormed and taken at this time to be extended. Probably even Eggardon and Pilsdon fell, strong as they are—but what of Badbury Ring, Hambledon, Rawlsbury, Weatherby Castle, Woodbury Hill, Cadbury Castle, Abbotsbury and the group to the west at Hembury, Musbury Castle, Seaton Down, Blackbury and Woodbury Castle, Castle Neroche, to mention only the most likely? Then there are the sites to the north like Bratton Castle, Battlesbury and Sidbury. But these may have been in the territory of the Belgae and can be included only if this was the second of the 'warlike tribes' to resist Vespasian's advance. There is also the chain of hill-forts along the Mendips, which would bring the total well beyond the modest twenty of Suetonius. Of Vespasian's campaign one thing seems very clear: the speed of the advance and weight of attack took the tribes by surprise, and this is shown by the examples of defences walls left in an unfinished state.

III

Until recently there was little archaeological evidence which could be linked with any certainty to Vespasian, apart from Maiden Castle and Hod Hill. Gradually pieces of the jig-saw have come to light and traces of a pattern are beginning to emerge. The mention by Suetonius of the Isle of Wight suggests that Vespasian may have planned his advance as a combined sea and land operation. With the assistance of the fleet, it would be possible to move supplies and heavy equipment with greater ease than by land. There were as yet no metalled roads. The army marched and rode along wide cleared lanes across the hills and forests, where hostile tribes could wage successful guerrilla action, as they were to do later in Wales. Sea transport would require secure bases, and the south coast abounds in land-locked harbours west of Bosham. One cannot however use the modern Admiralty Pilot to interpret the conditions of the first century. Many changes have taken place in the last 2,000 years; it is extremely difficult to assess the combined effects of land sinkage, marine erosion, and the growth of shingle banks, besides the large-scale dredging in Southampton Water and Portsmouth Harbour.[21] It is not unreasonable to assume that, different in shape and size as they may have been in the first century, a succession of harbours would have been available to the light-draught Roman transports. There is a little archaeological evidence for this. Many years ago a legionary helmet of mid-first-century type was dredged up in Bosham Harbour. It passed through several collections and eventually found a home in Lewes Museum.[22] An oyster shell is still fixed to the crest-knob and this is evidence of the helmet lying in estuarine waters after being lost overboard. In the Chichester Museum there is a small collection of military bronzes and pieces of equipment, formerly in the Sadler Collection, and a fine horse-pendant has been picked up on Lancing Down[23] (see Appendix III,

p. 185). The recent excavation of the remarkable villa at Fishbourne has revealed the presence of timber buildings of Claudian date below the later stone structures. The excavator has suggested that they may have been store-houses or granaries, part of a military base.[24] With this coastal area and large land-locked harbour in the friendly hands of Rome's ally Cogidubnus, it would hardly be surprising to find that Vespasian used Bosham as a base from which to advance.

Further evidence may come from the other great harbours, showing the fleet operating from a string of bases along the coast and bringing up supplies for the army as it marched westwards. One such base, probably a permanent one, appears to have been established at Hamworthy in Poole Harbour. The area is now a desolate waste of gravel pits and factories and any hopes of further discoveries have faded. Fortunately a local school took an interest in the site before it was completely despoiled and a few trenches produced pottery of this early date which is now in Poole Museum.[25] From this site came the donkey-mill which is the largest and most elaborate example of its kind from Britain and is now in the British Museum.[26] Another base was probably sited at Topsham in the estuary of the Exe where early pottery has been found, but nothing conclusive of military occupation.[27]

Of the inland forts not a great deal is yet known. Where they have been examined in detail they appear to be permanent in character and to have been occupied into the sixties. From their distribution it seems that a tight network of closely spaced units was made necessary by the nature of the terrain and continued hostility of its population. Only the fort at Hod Hill has been completely excavated. The British Museum contains a fine collection of objects from this site which had been assiduously gathered together by Henry Durden, a Blandford ironmonger in the last century, as they were brought up by the plough.[28] When Professor Richmond was asked to write an account of these antiquities he replied that this could not be done unless their full context could be investigated. The Trustees of the British Museum then took the unusual course of instigating an excavation, and asked him to direct it. The results of his eight seasons' work will soon appear in print[29] and will show a remarkable state of affairs. The very siting of a Roman fort in the corner of an

Iron Age hill-fort is most unusual: the normal situation is on lower ground at river crossings. Waddon, near Beaminster, is also on a hill, and if there is a fort at Ham Hill this may be a third. The reason for these anomalous sitings is the nature of the country, the absence of sizeable rivers and the hilly, broken ground which was probably thickly wooded and prevented the army from adopting its normal methods.

The plan of Hod Hill also shows peculiarities. Instead of the usual auxiliary unit, about 500 strong, there were two different kinds of troops—legionaries, and troopers of a cavalry *ala*. The final analysis of the garrison must await Professor Richmond's report, but there appears to be barrack provision for four centuries of legionaries (380 men) and ten troops of cavalry (320 men). Each unit would have its own commander, and that of the cavalry would have been the senior. There are two houses for these officers, the larger and more elaborate clearly belonging to the cavalry *praefectus*. This arrangement of putting two different kinds of unit together in the same fort is one which had serious dangers. At a later period when the fort of Newstead in Scotland was so provided, it was necessary to build a wall between the two units and give each a separate bath-house. Only in this way could quarrels and brawling be prevented.

This peculiarity of Hod Hill seems to be repeated at Waddon Hill near Beaminster, where six seasons of excavation have revealed the plans of three large buildings in the central area of the fort.[30] Although insufficient of the fort plan is as yet known, the pieces of equipment indicate the presence of legionaries and possibly also of auxiliaries, but this can only be adequately shown when the barrack-blocks are explored. Unfortunately at Waddon a substantial part of the fort has been removed by stone quarrying. Many objects and coins were found, some being acquired by Ralls, a Bridport corn-merchant, eventually to find their way into the Bridport Museum where they lay in a dark corner for many years, their significance unnoticed. The most interesting of these items is undoubtedly the fine dagger-scabbard first seen as a mass of rust, but recognised by its shape. After careful cleaning an inlaid pattern of gold-alloy emerged, but much of the detail had been lost (27).

The work on Waddon has produced a few details which help to

throw a light on the life of soldiers. For example, the bulk of the pottery used for cooking and eating was obtained from native potters. It consisted of typical Durotrigian bowls and jars in a black, highly burnished ware. But the troops also needed other vessels such as mixing-bowls (*mortaria*) and flagons—forms new to Britain. These were either imported, or else local potters were quick to imitate Romanised types. A kiln of this period was found at Corfe Mullen[31] not far from the base at Hamworthy mentioned above. The products were mostly *mortaria* and flagons but native-type jars and bowls were also made here. This shows that Corfe Mullen could hardly have been a works-depôt but rather the kiln of a Durotrigian potter successfully producing the kind of wares needed for this new market. Whether he operated under contract or duress it would be difficult to show. Rubbish pits inside the fort gave some indication of military diet—apart from the usual animal bones there were also those of fish, notably the Giant Wrasse, a very bony fish which modern anglers normally throw back into the sea. Of the 101 bones of hare, 81 are parts of the foot.[32] There is a large number of small black-and-white counters, relics possibly of gambling.

The sites of the other forts in the south-west have not yet been so convincingly demonstrated. The evidence for Ham Hill has already been cited[33] and the considerable collection of equipment must indicate the presence of a fort, unless these finds are part of a cache of loot. There is a small gravel plateau near Wiveliscombe about six miles due west of Taunton which is defended by ditches and rampart. In the style of fortification and choice of site commanding the valleys debouching from the Brendon Hills, this fort is typically Roman. Unfortunately the modest excavation of 1956 produced neither pottery nor equipment to clinch the issue.[34] A fort here would fit well into the strategic pattern of advanced posts half-way between Exeter and the mouth of the Parrett.

One of the important facts which emerges from a study of the early forts is that in many cases their sites later became civil settlements. The presence of troops would have attracted those natives who could see an opportunity of developing trade. Soldiers in foreign service the world over have human needs—food, drink, entertainment, women—which only civilians can supply. These

SCALE IN FEET

0   50   100   150   200

23   *Plan of the Claudian fort at Waddon Hill, Dorset, showing the timber buildings excavated up to 1964 (The hatched lines indicate the edge of the modern quarry)*

transactions flourished regardless of any feelings of hostility, and small civil settlements would have sprung up outside the forts. From these modest origins would develop the permanent towns, many of which survived the later movement of troops towards the north and west. In this area there are the Roman towns of Exeter, Dorchester, Ilchester, Camerton and Sea Mills, the first two being tribal capitals. It would be a reasonable assumption that they also began in the first century as forts, and if they are seen in relationship to the known military sites they seem consistent with the general pattern. This is equally true, as will be seen below, of the forts in the rest of the frontier zone. In the south-west, too, it seems quite certain that these towns could not have had any earlier origin: but in all these examples excavations have been on too small a scale to produce much direct evidence.

Exeter suffered serious damage during the last war; excavation has preceded some of the redevelopment and the results of this work have been published.[35] The earliest levels were found to be rich in pottery and glass of the Claudian period, but devoid of military equipment. This evidence is held to represent early civic development and since there is no trace of native settlement, this must indicate a Roman foundation. It seems unlikely that the Roman authorities would have established a tribal centre here on the very limit of the frontier while the area was under military control. Like so many of the towns, it is far more reasonable to suppose that this civil development came later when the army withdrew. This suggestion is supported by the coin evidence. The series is very strong for the reigns of Claudius to Vespasian and then tends to fall away, a situation comparable to Wroxeter. The absence of military equipment or structures is not so serious when it is realised that no archaeological investigations have yet been carried out on the plateau on which the cathedral stands. The geographer Ptolemy placed the IInd *Augusta* here, an interesting mistake in view of the possible military connections, but it seems clear that he was confusing the two places, Exeter and Caerleon, which had the same name (Isca), derived from the river. In any event, the legion would hardly be placed in such an exposed position on the frontier, and when military occupation is found it will probably be auxiliary in character. The superb quality of the silvered and niello-enamelled pieces from Ham Hill suggest the presence of legionaries in strength there, the most central position of the whole south-west frontier system.

Dorchester has produced a few items of equipment, including the bone sword-handle grip of a legionary *gladius* and a very fine enamelled belt-mount (*28*).[36] Doubtless the site of the fort will be found during the excavation of the Roman town, which probably spread over it. There is no evidence as yet from Ilchester or Camerton,[37] but at the latter the early construction of the Fosse Way seems to be confirmed. There must be other forts in the area, possibly somewhere near Axminster and Yeovil, awaiting discovery.[38]

The situation along the coast-line of the Bristol Channel would have been quite different from that of the south coast, since supplies brought by sea would face the long and difficult journey round Land's End. Forts in north-west Somerset are more likely to have been supplied by land routes from the south and east. The harbours along the Channel, however, had another part to play in later campaigns. As soon as a decision was taken to wage war on the Silures of South Wales, naval bases would be needed for reconnaissance, attack and ferrying troops and supplies across the Bristol Channel. This will be discussed below in the proper context. It is sufficient at this stage to note the two important harbour inlets, at Combwich at the mouth of the Parrett, and Sea Mills at the mouth of the Avon. The sea-level here has risen since Roman times and sites of that period are now found below the modern sea and water-table at places like Weston-super-Mare. Sites on higher ground will of course remain and there is a small Roman settlement at or near Combwich, whose late cemetery at Cannington with its thousands of burials has been excavated in recent years.[39] It seems possible that the Roman settlement developed outside an early fort. On the other hand, this is an obvious site for a small port and trading settlement. For Sea Mills there is better evidence, recovered from rather casual digging on a site which is now almost obliterated by housing development.[40] The early pottery, coins and military equipment are conclusive evidence of a fort or naval base; from the small later civil settlement, known as Abonae according to the Antonine Itinerary, a ferry service probably operated across the Bristol Channel.

24 The advance under Aulus Plautius and the frontier of A.D. 47

LEGEND:
▲ LEGIONARY FORTRESS
■ MILITARY SITE
● CIVIL SITE

GESORIACUM (Boulogne)

RUTUPIAE (Richborough)

(Colchester) CAMULODUNUM LEG. XX

(Fingringhoe Wick)

LEG. IX

LINDUM (Lincoln)

LEG. XIV (?)

VERULAMIUM (St. Albans)

THE MEDWAY BATTLE

ICENI

TRINOVANTES

CATUVELLAUNI

C O R I T A N I

NOVIOMAGUS (Chichester)

LEG. II AUG

COASTAL SQUADRONS SUPPLYING LAND FORCES

ATREBATES

RATAE (Leicester)

R. NENE

R. TRENT

FRONTIER ZONE

PLAUTIAN

CALLEVA (Silchester)

CORINIUM (Cirencester)

DOBUNNI

R. AVON

VECTIS

(Hamworthy)

D U R O T R I G E S

GLEVUM (Gloucester)

(Topsham)

SCALE IN MILES

0 10 20 40 60 80 100

It should be clear from this survey that the archaeological traces of the conquest and subsequent occupation of the south-west, although faint, are certain enough for a pattern to be distinguished and even for some conclusions to emerge. The gaps in our knowledge are, however, very large. Many more discoveries are needed before we can interpret the work of Vespasian, or understand the problems which faced the military authorities in maintaining large forces in this hostile area. We do not yet know how long this was necessary, nor whether the units were withdrawn at the same time or by stages.

IV

The evidence of archaeology is the only guide for the advance to the midlands and the north since there are no biographical details of the commanders involved. Before any forward move could be made, Aulus Plautius, that prudent general, established a strong base in the rear at Colchester, with easy access to the sea and the mouth of the Rhine. The evidence for the army at Camulodunum appears in Tacitus, who refers to the later establishment of the *colonia* in terms to suggest that freeing a legion was its object. There are also two military tombstones found separately near Beverley Road (*2, 4*).[41] One is of M. Favonius Facilis, a centurion of the XXth Legion, and shows in relief a grim-visaged officer holding his vine stick, a symbol of rank, with one hand, while the other rests on the pommel of his sword slung on his left. His dress and armour are seen in fine detail, down to the highly decorated belt-plate. The stone proclaims his authority and there is a clear touch of arrogance in his stance. To stand before this monument in Colchester Museum is to begin to understand something of the might of Rome, and to feel a measure of compassion for the free Celtic warriors being crushed by such assurance and efficiency. The other stone, of equal interest, is that of an auxiliary horseman, Longinus of the First Thracian *ala*.[42] He was the son of Sdapezematygus and came from Sardica, which is now Sofia in Bulgaria. He wears a jerkin of large bronze scales (*lorica squamata*), carries an oval shield and rides a well-groomed horse which strides over a naked hairy foe cowering in terror like Caliban.

Both these stones appear to have belonged to a small military cemetery along a Roman road which ran approximately from east to west, but a quarter of a mile south of the *colonia*. It seems therefore to have been associated with an early road system, which must have been based on the military site yet to be found. The two tombstones were broken and defaced by the British rebels at the time of the Boudiccan revolt in A.D. 60.[43] There is evidence from Fingringhoe, which lies in the estuary of the River Colne, that this may have been the site of a military store-base with direct access to the mouth of the old Rhine, where military activity of this period has been attested.[44]

To the south and east of Severn and Trent the only tribes which escaped the domination of the Catuvellauni were the Iceni of East Anglia and the Durotriges of Dorset, both of too tough and independent spirit to fall before the Belgic Kingdom. The Iceni remained independent for the time being; the implacable Durotriges were battered into surrender by the IInd *Augusta*. A section of the Dobunni to the west, as we have seen, seem to have succumbed to the Catuvellauni and were quick to ally themselves to Rome.

The position of the other midland tribe, the Coritani, is more difficult to assess. This people appear to have occupied the eastern watershed of the Trent and to have included the modern shires of Lincoln, Leicester and Rutland. If this was indeed the tribal area, the Trent seems to have been a political divide. To the east in Lincolnshire there is growing evidence of Belgic influence and the centre of this may have been Old Sleaford, where traces of a mint have been found. On the Humber at South Ferriby Belgic pottery indicates a settlement or trading-post. Beyond the Trent, apart from a few coins in Yorkshire, there are only hoards, buried perhaps by refugees or traders. The Coritanian coins[45] form a common frontier with those of the Iceni along the River Nene and extend to the south-west to the divide between the watersheds of Trent and Avon. The peoples west of the Trent appear to be a mixture of earlier cultures unaffected by Belgic influence. It is doubtful if Leicester was a pre-Roman settlement since all the early pottery on which this supposition is based could well have been introduced by the army.[46] The tribe may originally have been confined to the territories east of the Trent and subject to Belgic overlords. When the Romans later organised Britain into a province the more backward tribes west of the river

25   *A legionary helmet, dredged up from the Thames*

26   *A large gilded bronze horse-pendant, with a stylised bird-mount, found at Cirencester*

27 *Part of a dagger scabbard from the fort on Waddon Hill, Dorset*

28 *A bronze buckle, decorated with millefiore inlay, from Dorchester, Dorset*

29 *A bronze mess-tin from Gloucester*

MILITARY EQUIPMENT

may have been added to form the *civitas Coritanorum*. The siting of the capital at Leicester, so far from the apparent centre of its tribal area, may have been influenced by the creation of the *colonia* at Lincoln, and perhaps by the designation of the Fens as a special development area or Imperial domain.

Aulus Plautius probably advanced into these regions from Colchester with circumspection, leaving forts in his rear. For a short time at least it was deemed prudent to have a fort at Verulamium, the old capital of the Catuvellauni. There has been found, buried underneath the town's late second-century bank but overlying Belgic occupation, a typical military rampart revetted in timber.[47] This accords with items of military equipment found in excavations in the Roman town and nearby. A legionary helmet of this early period was found in 1813 when the Grand Junction Canal was being cut at Northcott Hill.[48] A punched inscription on the neck-guard indicates that one of its owners was a legionary of the first cohort. The legion concerned is probably the XIVth, which advanced north-west along the line of Watling Street, eventually to reach Wroxeter.

The other legion involved in the advance was the IXth. Its route may be judged by the fact that it became established at Lincoln. This force, then, advanced in a northerly direction, skirting the boundaries of the Icenian kingdom and the Fens, yet to be drained. Dr St Joseph has found a large fort about half legionary size near Longthorpe on the Nene and this may well mark a halting place. This river, as mentioned above, was probably the southern boundary of the Coritani, and the attitude of this tribe to the Romans may at this stage have been uncertain. If it was known how long this fort was occupied an estimate of the situation might be attempted. Again, if sufficient datable material could be recovered from the earliest levels at Lincoln, it might be possible to determine when the legion arrived there. At present, in the absence of evidence to the contrary, it can be assumed that a cautious general might have paused at the Nene at this significant stage of the advance. It does however seem fairly certain that the territory of the Coritani was to be wholly occupied by the army. The first example of this to be noted is the fort established on the south side of the river Nene protecting the crossing near the later town of Durobrivae (Water Newton).[49] It may be noted also that there is some slight evidence of a Roman fort at Cambridge in the form of a ditch yielding Claudian pottery[50] under the Shire Hall, which if substantiated may also mark a halting place along the line of advance —unless of course it belongs to the later troubles of A.D. 60.

Gradually, then, the army moved into its forward area, legions and *auxilia* alike. Until the sites of more forts are known it is impossible to consider in detail the basic pattern of the new frontier created by Aulus Plautius. Up to a few years ago no one was quite sure that it even existed, but thanks mainly to air photography it is possible to glimpse the situation. The Roman governor had to deal with a problem for which there was little precedent. The main imperial frontiers laid down by Augustus had definite physical boundaries. To the west was the Atlantic, to the north the great rivers Rhine and Danube, to the east the deserts of Parthia, and to the south the greater desert of the Sahara. In regions of uncertainty, client kingdoms were set up as buffer states. Behind these lines the Roman Army was thinly stretched, but units were usually grouped together in large camps— a survival of the earlier idea of winter quarters. The method is well illustrated by Caesar's campaigns in Gaul, where after the summer campaigns the general carefully placed his legions to winter where they could be well supplied, keep an eye on the uncertain tribes, and be easily brought together in an emergency. In these winter quarters the troops bivouacked under their leather tents, and the whole arrangement was considered to be a temporary one. In the east, where there were urban civilisations older than that of Rome, the solution was easier, for the troops were merely quartered in the cities. As the frontiers became firmly established and the districts now within the Empire pacified, it was natural for the army to winter along the frontier itself. But by now the soldiers had years of bitter experience of attempting to camp out in the winters of north-western Europe. The attempts to dig drainage channels round the tents to prevent the camp from being completely waterlogged are seen at the site of Hofheim near Wiesbaden. At some period—probably under the old warrior Tiberius whose knowledge of these conditions from personal experience was greater than that of Augustus— the *hiberna* gave place to the permanent fort with its wooden barracks, stores and other buildings. By A.D. 43 the practice was well established and the tented camp was normally a feature only of summer campaigns. The development in the planning of internal arrangements from tents to permanent wooden buildings was still in progress, however, and presents some fascinating problems. Because tents can be easily pitched and struck the internal planning of the *hiberna* tended to be a loose affair with merely a rough division of barrack areas, horse lines, through-ways and store and waggon parks. The commander's tent was pitched in the centre and the others grouped around it. So it is hardly surprising to find in the early timber forts a lack of rigid planning. The Claudian forts in Britain show great variety, both in general planning and the internal arrangement of buildings, which makes it often difficult to offer a precise identification of each. The effect of this is to make these early forts extremely interesting to excavate and quite unlike the stereotyped planning which had become established by the end of the first century. It is possible, for example, in the forts of Agricola, to identify and plot the buildings by cutting a series of trenches across them in a reasonably economical manner; the Claudian forts require a much more extensive investigation before they can be understood.

In looking for the sites of early forts there is—as we have seen— a very useful indication in the presence of a Roman civil settlement. This applies especially in the frontier zone itself, but not exclusively so, since some of the Roman towns in the south-east, such as Camulodunum, Canterbury, Verulamium, Silchester and probably Winchester, began as native settlements.

V

Bearing this general pattern in mind, it is possible to make a tentative map of the forts in the frontier laid down by Aulus Plautius (*24*). It soon becomes clear that it represents defence in depth in a strip of country some thirty miles wide, occupied by army units. As suggested above, this may not so much be for protection against a frontal assault as to occupy the territories of tribes of uncertain allegiance. The forward position rests on the estuary of the Exe, the shore of the Bristol Channel, the lower Severn, the Warwickshire Avon, the

Trent and the Humber. That this represents the limit of the Plautian system is shown by the famous comment of Tacitus in describing the activities of the next Governor, Ostorius Scapula, who, when forced to advance still further, is said to have 'disarmed the suspected tribes and established control over the area on this side [i.e. the Roman side] of Trent and Severn'.[51] The road known as the Fosse Way has long been recognised as a military conception;[52] it now appears not as the *limes* itself, but as a lateral line of communication affording protected access to all parts of the frontier zone. One must here accept the continuation of the same military road north of Lincoln to the Humber, striding along the Lincoln Edge.[53] There is a growing body of archaeological evidence to support the argument suggested above. Of the two legions the movements of the IXth are clear. Those of the XIVth remain in doubt. This latter legion must have been established for a few years in the central section of the frontier but there is yet no hint as to where this may be.

The presence of the IXth at Lincoln is well attested by tombstones of its soldiers and investigations of its defences. The legion was probably here by *c.* A.D. 46–7 and remained until A.D. 71. During this time the fort seems to have remained forty-two acres in extent instead of the normal legionary size of fifty to sixty acres.[54] This suggests that about a tenth of the unit, perhaps six centuries, approximating to an auxiliary unit, was posted elsewhere. As the fortress lies deeply buried below the later Roman town and its medieval and modern successors, it has never been possible to examine any area within its defences, and any future excavation may have to be limited by these factors. Investigation of the defences has given enough information to reconstruct them (*30*).[55] The rampart was a modest size, twelve feet wide with the usual row of timbers laid down at right angles to form a foundation. At the front was a timber revetment securely placed in a foundation trench; at the back was a slighter construction which probably held up only the lower three or four feet. Traces of an inner ditch of normal size have been noted, and there were presumably at least two of these.

So far there is no evidence of military sites of this period north of Lincoln, but it will undoubtedly be found. To the south of the legionary fortress there are traces along the Fosse Way. At Brough, where a small settlement known as Crococalana later developed, a fine bronze cheek-piece of an auxiliary trooper's parade helmet has been found (*31*).[56] The next site to the south is Ad Pontem (Thorpe-by-Newark) where there must have been a bridge across the Trent

30 *Westgate, Lincoln: reconstruction of the defences of the legionary fortress*

constructed when pacification had been established. Here there is a complexity of crop-marks suggestive of defences: evidence of a fort has been found in a recent excavation.[57] Further along still an anomalous situation exists at Margidunum (Castle Hill),[58] where the apparent remains of a Claudian fort with internal stone buildings have been published. It now seems quite clear in the light of new knowledge that the area investigated was part of the civil settlement, and the fort probably lies on the higher ground to the north-east. For some time the peculiar polygonal plan of this supposed fort has been accepted as an example of irregular planning at this period.[59]

We propose to say nothing of the stamped tile of the VIIIth (?) Legion at Leicester, nor of other stamped tiles elsewhere, since it seems fairly certain that none of the legions in Britain began stamping tiles until much later.

There are, however, two possible fort sites in advance of the Fosse in this sector. One is where a unit might be expected to protect a crossing of the Trent—at Littleborough, four miles south of Gainsborough. A well-defined Roman road, now known as Till Bridge Lane, branches from Ermine Street and heads north, offering an alternative route to the crossing of the Humber and to York. This must have been the main Roman highway to the north in a later context. It appears in the Antonine Itinerary, and there would probably have been a bridge here at that time. This is however one of the Roman routes which has fallen into disuse—probably after the collapse of the bridge—the crossing at Gainsborough being preferred since the time of the Danes. The Roman settlement of Segelocum was established on the west bank of the Trent, but the fort is most likely to have been on the other side. Stukeley has an enigmatic note 'On the east side of the river has been a camp',[60] but whatever earthworks he may have seen or heard about have now vanished under the plough. The other fort site is at Broxstowe beyond the Trent, and is now obliterated by a council housing estate on the north-western outskirts of Nottingham. Earthworks have been noted here and some sporadic excavations, rather ill-recorded, did produce Claudian pottery and coins, and also some military equipment which was not identified at the time.[61]

There are no other known forts of this period in Lincolnshire, but the siting of the little towns at Caistor and Horncastle suggests military planning. This may of course belong to a much later period. A fort may be expected at Ancaster where a Roman town (Causennae) later developed;[62] probably also at Old Sleaford, where recent discoveries have indicated the existence of a Belgic centre of some

31 *A decorated cheek-piece of a cavalry parade helmet, found at Crococalana (Brough in Nottingham-shire)*

32 *An iron ring, with intaglio of eagle and standards, found at the fort at Great Casterton, Rutland*

33 *Crop-marks of the Roman forts at Great Casterton, Rutland*

importance. On the two routes between Ancaster and Durobrivae there is one known fort at Great Casterton, at the crossing of the Gwash on the western limb. Here a series of summer schools, directed by Dr Philip Corder, explored the defences of the small Roman town and a villa nearby.[63] Early pottery and a piece of military equipment gave advance warning of the presence of a fort. In spite of intensive searching and discussion of the problem, it was only after the school had closed down that the fort was discovered in the field next to that in which much of the excavation had taken place. Under exceptional circumstances crop-marks had developed and Dr St Joseph observed and photographed the unmistakable outlines of two forts, one within the other (*33*).[64] Although much of this site had been open and available for excavation while the school was in operation, new bungalows were now being built across the northern part of it. Two further seasons of excavation were carried out by some of the students of the previous schools under Professor I. A. Richmond. Sufficient pottery was recovered to establish a Claudian date for the military occupation. The ditch of the reduced fort had at a later date been considerably enlarged by doubling its depth, going well into the solid limestone.[65] Among the finds was a turf-cutter, very like one in any modern ironmonger's shop, and a fine intaglio for a ring which may have been worn by a centurion, showing the standards and an eagle (*32*). Two periods of timber buildings were clearly discernible; with work on a larger scale it would be possible to obtain the plans of the two forts in the area free of the road and modern houses.

In the central part of the Fosse frontier, between Leicester and Cirencester, no military sites are known. This is probably due, as we shall see, to the fact that this sector was vacated in A.D. 48–9. Even so there must have been forts in this area; doubtless they will be found. In any attempt to locate them the sites of the civil settlements should be the first to be considered. High Cross (Venonae) is situated at the junction of the Fosse Way and Watling Street and is clearly a site of major strategic importance. It is remarkable that no hint of military occupation has come from air photography, from casual finds, or from the excavations made necessary by road widening. There is certainly a considerable spread of civil occupation around the junction of the Roman roads, but the pottery does not seem to be earlier than *c.* A.D. 70. The next site to the south along Watling Street is Caves Inn (Tripontium), but it is unfortunate that most of the site had been removed by gravel working before any detailed investigation could be made. Among the many objects found during these operations is a fine military mess-tin,[66] identical with others of the Claudian period. Much mid-first-century pottery has turned up at Duston and Kettering[67] and this may also represent the passage of the army—if it is not the result of earlier Belgic intrusion. Of the other settlement sites such as Irchester, Whilton Lodge (Bannaventa), Towcester (Lactodorum), Chesterton (on the Fosse) and Dorn, so little work has been done that it is hardly surprising that nothing has yet been found. Alchester in Oxfordshire has been partly excavated and produced an early type of harness clip.[68]

For one of the advance posts in this sector a possible site is Alcester on the Alne, a tributary of the Warwickshire Avon. But in spite of extensive investigation over the past few years no sign of occupation as early as this has appeared. A harness ring with a masked loop, like those used by an auxiliary cavalry,[69] is a useful incentive. The next sign of anything military is thirty miles to the north-east at Mancetter (Manduessedum) on Watling Street. There are two quite different sites here. The Roman town lies astride the road, while a mile away in a much better tactical position is the small hamlet of Mancetter with its fine church and manor house. Stukeley visited this site in the company of the great Warwickshire map-maker Henry Beighton and records a deeply entrenched camp 'but I cannot say with so much regularity as to its present appearance that will ascertain it to the Romans'. There the matter might have remained but for two recent discoveries. A bank by the Almshouses was examined by Mr Adrian Oswald in 1955 when working on the Roman civil site. Although this bank was found to be medieval, it sealed a Roman ditch with Claudian pottery in it.[70] Since then, a small hoard of coins of Claudius has been found in digging a drain, and taken together these finds clearly indicate the presence here of a Roman fort. This is a site which would repay further investigation.

Between the central area and the south-west, the problems of which have already been discussed, there lie the Cotswolds and the valley of the lower Severn. A key position must have been the junction of Avon and Severn. The best site here is the narrow angle between the two rivers where there is now a motte and bailey castle, showing its tactical importance. But nine miles to the south is Gloucester, where military activity is certain. However, the evidence at present is confusing. There are at least two distinct sites, at Kingsholm to the north-east of the city, and below the medieval city itself. The Kingsholm site has in the past decade been much built over and large-scale investigation is no longer possible. During the early nineteenth century much metalwork was found, probably by the plough, and this was illustrated and discussed by that indefatigable Gloucestershire antiquary Samuel Lysons.[71] These objects were placed in the British Museum, but time has not dealt kindly with the ironwork and little survives, although the finest item, a bronze mess-tin,[72] is still in splendid condition. There are a few more objects in the Gloucester Museum. It is not possible to identify the troops who occupied this site, though some of the equipment (such as the pioneer axe-head sheaths and what may be a *pilum*-head) were used by legionaries. Investigations in recent years have not been fruitful[73] and so doubt has been cast on the idea that Kingsholm was ever occupied by a Roman legion.[74] The finds recorded by Lysons, and early coins and pottery since his day, together with the behaviour of the Roman road system, all strongly indicate the presence here of a unit of the army. This may have been the Thracian cohort commemorated by the tombstone of Rufus Sita now in the Gloucester Museum. The XXth Legion was moved to Gloucester as a result of a situation which forms part of the later history of the frontier and is discussed below. Now that it is known that military defences underlie those of the civil *colonia*[75] it is possible to think of this as the site of the legionary fortress. As happened at Lincoln, the colony may have replaced the military base with precisely the same *enceinte*.

Another site which has received much attention of recent years is Cirencester. Progress is disfiguring this once lovely Cotswold town, the site of a large and important Roman city. The opportunity for excavation so provided has been taken by Mr John Wacher, and he has added much new material. The town has long been known to have early military connections. There are two fine cavalry tombstones in the Museum of troopers of two different auxiliary units, an *ala Indiana*[76] and an *ala Thracum*.[77] The latter is the finer of the two and shows the caparison in some detail; although his face is damaged it seems probable that the trooper was wearing a parade helmet with a face-mask and carries a standard which appears to be folded (*5*). Although the armour is quite different from that of the Colchester stone it is possible that it was the same unit: the difference may be that of rank. A third tombstone, found near these two at about the same time, appears to be of an equally early date but commemorates a civilian, one Philus of the Sequani, a tribe in the upper Saône valley in east Gaul. This man was possibly a trader who followed in the wake of the army.[78] Among the objects found in the town, and which are now in the Museum collection, are over a dozen pieces of military equipment, some clearly belonging to the cavalry, such as the remarkable gilded chest-plate with a bird mount (*26*).[79] Until 1961, the site of the fort was a matter of speculation. In that year, however, Mr Wacher, in his excavations to west of the Basilica of the Forum, found the defences, consisting of two ditches, a turf rampart, and traces of timber buildings of three periods inside the fort.[80] A remarkably fortunate discovery was a large quantity of pottery, thrown into the inner ditch when the site was abandoned and levelled out. Surplus supplies from the quartermaster's stores were literally ditched. This helps to establish a terminal date which seems to be not earlier than *c.* A.D. 60–5; but if the pottery was by then old stock and so discarded, it may be somewhat later.

Little can be said of any other sites to the south of Cirencester but it would seem possible that some of the civil settlements like Mildenhall (Cunetio), Sandy Lane (Verlucio), Wanborough (Durocornovium) and White Walls may have had a military origin. So also might Bath (Aquae Sulis), as the potentialities of the hot springs were quickly developed.[81] Among the inscriptions of those who sought the waters are some belonging to soldiers, but they must be of a later period.

Thus the pattern of the military frontier devised by the first Governor, Aulus Plautius, begins to take shape, although at present it is ill-defined in places. The Governor had reason to be satisfied with his arrangements, for he had completed in a thoroughly workmanlike manner the task to which he had been assigned. The addition of the British lowlands to the Empire, begun so inauspiciously by the great Julius, was now complete. An awkward legacy inherited by Augustus was tidied up in a most satisfactory manner. Aulus Plautius, his term of office having expired, could retire to Rome and enjoy his *ovatio*.[82] This 'lesser triumph' was a distinction by then almost never awarded outside the Imperial family, to which Aulus Plautius was indeed connected by marriage. A triumph for the Emperor, but merely *triumphalia ornamenta* for victorious generals, had become the practice. Both Claudius' antiquarianism and his sense of the value of Aulus Plautius' work in Britain are attested by this revival of the *ovatio* for a senator after an interval of sixty-six years. The attention accorded by the Emperor in coming out of the city to meet the returning Governor, and in conceding him the place of honour in the ascent to the Capitol, aroused much comment. The whole affair will have served to keep the conquest of Britain before the public gaze.[83]

But however satisfied Claudius and his ministers may have been at the outcome, there were others less content. The elder Pliny records that the possibility of large new sources of silver in Britain, of which there must have been an inkling, caused perturbation among the owners and lessees of the Spanish silver mines, some of which were by now becoming very deep, and where extraction of the ore was being made difficult by flooding.[84] Fearing a sudden reduction in the price of silver, the proprietors of the mines attempted to place restrictions on the British output. Although Caesar had told Cicero that there was no silver in Britain, this may have been as an excuse for not pursuing his plans of conquest. It may have been the development of British coinage that started the first serious search for silver deposits, though it seems that the Romans knew of the Mendip ores. A stamped lead pig datable to A.D. 49[85] shows that silver extraction was in full swing five years after the landing. The fact that the inscription on the pig includes the letters 'DE BRITAN' suggests that the silver and lead were both exportable commodities; this rapid assault on the mineral wealth of Britain implies a strong economic motive for the conquest.

Ostorius Scapula
and the Campaign in Wales
A.D. 47–51

5

The second Governor of Britain did not find it a rewarding assignment. Nothing is known of the earlier career of Ostorius Scapula.
We can deduce a military reputation, but do not know where it was
gained. He held the consulship some time earlier than A.D. 45. In the
autumn of 47 he crossed to Britain to find the province in a state of
turmoil which he never wholly suppressed, despite his great achievement of defeating Caratacus in Wales.

For the campaigns against Caratacus in Wales and their prelimin-
aries Tacitus is the only historical source. Archaeology can offer
supplementary evidence, but this, as will be seen later, is seldom
clear or precisely datable. It is therefore important to know what
limitations and conventions the use of Tacitus must impose. His
account of the Claudian invasion, and (presumably) the events in
Britain under Aulus Plautius, will have come in one of the lost Books
of the *Annals*. It will have told of Caratacus' movements after his
defeat at the Medway, and of the position he was able to win among
the tribes of Wales. The narrative we have[1] carries an account of
British affairs from A.D. 47 to 57, under Ostorius Scapula and Didius
Gallus. The unwarlike Didius Gallus (as Tacitus portrays him) comes
only in the last of nine chapters, and seven of the others are given
over to the Caratacus episode, which covers four years (A.D. 47–51).
Selective and highly compressed, much is omitted; two episodes are
chosen for special treatment. These are Caratacus' final battle, and
his speech at the military review in Rome which marked his surrender. They occupy four chapters and part of a fifth. Two chapters
only are devoted to Ostorius' first three years in Britain. If, then,
Caratacus seems to emerge suddenly from the mists of Wales in the
autumn of the year 47, the impression is due to the accident which
deprived us of the earlier part of Tacitus' narrative.

LEGIONARY FORTRESS
■ **MILITARY SITE**
● **CIVIL SITE**

SCALE IN MILES

ICENI

CAMULODUNUM
(Colchester)

VERULAMIUM
(St. Albans)

BRIGANTES

CORITANI

LINDUM (Lincoln)
LEG. IX

PLAUTIAN FRONTIER ZONE

LEG. XIV (?)

VIROCONIUM
(Wroxeter)

CORNOVII

GLEVUM
(Gloucester)
LEG. XX

DECEANGLI

Campaign
into Flintshire

ORDOVICES

Site of
Battle (?)

Western limit of the
Frontier of Ostorius (?)

Thrust up the
Wye(?)

SILURES

LEG. II

Signal stations

COASTAL
SQUADRONS

34 *The advance under
Ostorius Scapula*

Conjecture is the sole source, and a bold and ingenious conjecture has recently been made to identify one phase of Caratacus' operations before he crossed the Severn into Wales.[2] North of Nailsworth and Minchinhampton, a tongue of the Cotswolds thrusts boldly towards the Stroud valley, forming a peninsula of hilly land two miles long and one mile across, and rising to 700 feet. This naturally strong defensive position contains Amberley Camp, a hill-fort of the Iron Age 'C' type, and its neck is cut off by The Bulwarks, a running earthwork resembling the Belgic dykes of the Colchester region. Here, it has been suggested, was the stronghold of Caratacus, from which he launched his attacks on the territory of the allies of Rome—especially on the lands of those of the Dobunni who had come to terms. Yet, if archaeological affinities point one way, military probability surely points the other. It can hardly be supposed that Aulus Plautius would leave the defiant Belgic king at large so close—barely a dozen miles—to the Roman *limes*, and free to range at will into territory so recently subdued. Equally, Caratacus must have been concerned to place himself beyond the reach of Rome while he mustered forces and supplies to renew the struggle. For both purposes, a link with the Brigantes was crucial. Wales, and not necessarily South Wales, is the logical choice.

By A.D. 47, when he comes once more into focus in the pages of Tacitus, Caratacus had clearly become the chosen war-leader of a confederacy of peoples hostile to Rome. Such a position, implying a supra-tribal military authority, was held by many great princes of the Celtic world—Cassivellaunus against Caesar in Britain, Vercingetorix, on a much greater scale, in Gaul. Such, later, was the position of Boudicca in the rebellion of A.D. 60. Approved by the chieftains of each of the tribes concerned, the war-leader wielded powers that were superior but neither absolute nor unquestioned. Skill in diplomacy and success in battle were needed to maintain them. Since the Druids, from their headquarters in Mona, were steadfast in hostility to Rome, we have deduced that their influence in the choice of Caratacus is highly probable. How far his direct military authority extended is not clear. Tacitus makes it plain that it was recognised by the Silures, Ordovices and Deceangli; of the attitude of the Demetae we know nothing, but it is hardly likely that they, alone of the tribes in Wales, could have been against him. Geographically, a key position was occupied by the Cornovii, in the gap between the hills of north-east Wales and the Peak. Whether that tribe was a coherent political entity at this period is uncertain, but at least some of them would seem to have supported Caratacus, to judge from reactions on the Roman side. In short, it would appear that Caratacus was in control of an area almost identical with that claimed for himself by Owen Glyndwr in the Tripartite Indenture of 1403.[3] Diplomatically, his influence will have extended further. The unsettled tribal politics of the Brigantes were troubled waters to fish; there was also discontent among the Iceni. In the old Belgic kingdom many hopes must have turned to Caratacus, especially from those who felt the rough edge of Roman rule. Indeed, he must have been a rallying point for all those elements in the province who, in Tacitus' words, 'spurned the Roman peace'.

The account of Tacitus suggests that Caratacus had established this position of military and diplomatic strength by A.D. 47. A state of hostility already exists. The change of governors provides the opportunity for a concerted attack on the territory of friendly tribes, under a central direction which must surely be his. The invaders are joined by tribes within the province itself: discontent is so widespread that the Roman Governor decides to disarm the tribes as soon as he is able to do so. The problem is to identify the territory invaded. Tacitus provides no place-names but a clue may be found in the comment on the methodical strategy of Ostorius, who 'held fast to his plan, and did not undertake new enterprises until the ground behind him was firmly consolidated'. As the plan unfolds itself its successive stages are seen to be: first, the expulsion of the invaders, second, the disarming of the tribes, and, third, the advance of the Roman *limes* up to the middle Severn. At this point Ostorius is diverted to deal with an outbreak of rebellion among the Iceni, supported by their neighbours. Once the position in East Anglia is stabilised, his next move is against the Deceangli of Flintshire.[4] The inference seems clear. The lands invaded will certainly include those of the Dobunni, between the Cotswolds and the Severn, which could be attacked from Silurian territory. But the Coritani seem also to be affected, if they were one of the neighbouring tribes which supported the rebellion of the Iceni, some months later. Cornovian territory would be the natural base for an assault on them, and this would account for the Roman decision to bring under control the 'midland triangle' between Severn and Trent, a decision which was to add just over one thousand square miles to the Roman province. Further, that Ostorius saw as his next step a punitive expedition against the Deceangli suggests that the epicentre of the whole assault on the Roman frontier lay on this north-eastern border of Wales. It is here, then, that we should expect to find Caratacus in the last months of the year 47.

Although Caratacus had made a shrewd choice of the moment to attack, he underestimated the speed and force of the Roman reaction. Ostorius quickly assembled a force of auxiliary troops for a counter-offensive; the enemy concentrations were dispersed, and invaders chased out of the province. Before the end of 47, the immediate menace was dispelled. Awkward problems lay ahead. Caratacus himself would have to be chastened, and further incursions into the province made impossible. The inadequacy of Aulus Plautius' line of frontier was now evident. It put the Romans too far east to come to grips with an enemy operating from Wales. It left far too much of the central midlands in hands that were hostile, or potentially so. A firm grip on the east bank of the Severn, from Gloucester to Wroxeter, had become imperative. To the north-east of this, the line of the Trent offered another natural barrier that would prolong a new frontier to the Humber. To advance thus far would be the logical next step; now that the relevant passage of Tacitus has been satisfactorily emended (see p. 102 above, and p. 4, note 51) we can see that Ostorius took it.

But the alarming intransigence of some of the tribes within the province would also have to be brought under control. To this end Ostorius decided to disarm all unreliable elements, a category in which he chose to include the Iceni, despite their status as a client-kingdom. It was a high-handed action, and the response was predictable. The Iceni—or a part of them—turned to war, joined by other rebels who had perhaps remained under arms since the previous autumn. East Anglia is not the territory for guerrilla warfare, but the leaders of the rebellion had provided themselves with a redoubt—a

SCALE IN FEET

0   500   1000   1:1500

35   *The Roman military sites at Greensforge, near Wolverhampton*

place, in the words of Tacitus 'protected by a rude earthwork, and with a narrow approach route, so as to be impenetrable to cavalry'. Its site has never been identified. Ostorius himself commanded the Roman force, which consisted of auxiliary infantry and cavalry: the legions, it would seem, had been disposed to watch any move by Caratacus. The cavalry, as such, could not be brought into operation, but the troopers were dismounted and joined the infantry in a general assault. The Britons were surrounded and caught in a trap of their own making. They were overcome after a desperate resistance. These operations in East Anglia and the midlands will probably have occupied the summer of A.D. 48.

II

The archaeological evidence for the activity of Ostorius in the midland triangle is at present very thin. Only a few sites have been investigated, and that on a limited scale. Where work has been done on the military sites in this area it has become increasingly evident that they have a history complicated by the continual troop movements backwards and forwards in the decade A.D. 50–60. Most of them have at least two if not three permanent forts on the same or nearby sites, and there are indications of temporary marching camps.

In some cases it seems that the earliest military fort is a large one, followed by a considerable reduction. This suggests groups of units probing forward in the initial stages, and smaller holding forces being left behind to consolidate the gain. A good example of this type of site is at Metchley in Birmingham, much of it now covered by parts of the Queen Elizabeth Hospital and the University Medical School.[5] The larger fort was sixteen acres and the smaller six and a quarter acres. Excavation of a corner tower of the earlier fort has shown the great timber uprights of the tower were taken out by driving trenches into the rampart from the front and the back. Later these open trenches collected a mass of charcoal representing the burning of the brush-wood and small timbers. In a recent piece of civic enterprise, the whole corner tower was rebuilt much as it must have been originally, but a losing battle was then engaged with the local youth who found this a heaven-sent target for destructive games, and no amount of fencing and barbed wire could keep them out. The whole site will soon be swallowed up by further hospital development, but recent investigations inside the earlier and larger fort show no traces of timber buildings and it seems probable that this well-fortified enclosure merely housed tents, and was now an intermediate type of site between the temporary marching camp and the permanent fort. It is logical to suppose that groups of units moving forward towards the enemy would not have been provided with buildings, since their fort would be a mere halting place. What is interesting is that the army felt insecure enough to dig in very thoroughly and erect elaborate corner towers. This suggests that Caratacus was falling back slowly to the Severn behind a screen of skirmishes or that his guerrilla bands were still very active.

A further eleven miles to the north-west from Metchley brings us to Greensforge where an earthwork was known for a long time as 'Wolverhampton Old Churchyard', a local attempt to explain its origin. A trench was cut across this in 1928 by a party of boys from Wolverhampton Grammar School and a useful section, with the pottery, was published in a manner admirable for its day.[6] Since then aerial photographs have shown that this fort was preceded by a larger marching camp, and another fort about the same size lies in the next field;[7] there are also traces of ditches and other features between the two forts. The photograph of the new fort even shows the post-holes of a gate and corner tower, and also a row of large pits behind the rampart which may be associated with its demolition. Much work is needed before the problems of these sites can be solved and the forts and camps fitted into the historical framework. There are similar complications at the little village of Wall, near Lichfield. Here a small but devoted band of amateurs has been excavating almost continuously over the last eight years, revealing more and yet more problems. The site is on Watling Street, one of the main lines of the Roman advance, and the district has long been known for the remains of Roman buildings. These belonged to the civil town of Letocetum; two of its principal buildings, the bath-house and probable *mansio* or hostelry, were found in 1912.[8] The former was studied in more detail in 1956.[9] The little town seems to occupy an area of five to ten acres, but so far its limits have not been

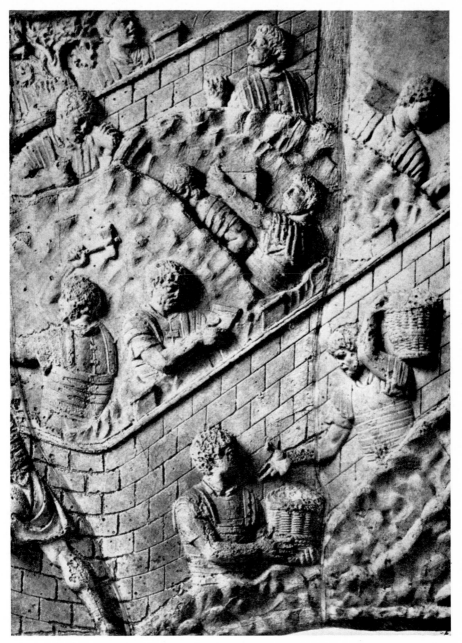

36 *Roman soldiers building a rampart with spoil from the
ditch between turf revetments at front and back*
From Trajan's Column

37 *The fort at Duncot, north of Wroxeter*

38 *Military site at Red Hill, near Oakengates, Shropshire*

ROMAN MILITARY SITES REVEALED BY CROP-MARKS

defined. Nor is there any trace of the defences which are usually such a marked feature of these settlements. Three parallel ditches have been observed from the air by Dr St Joseph,[10] but they turn out to belong to a small walled enclosure[11] of the fourth century straddling the Roman road, and excavations have produced no evidence of any substantial building inside; exactly what the function of this defensive work was—either in military or civil terms—it is difficult to understand. It was during the investigation of these late defences that remains were found of the earlier military phases. The few pieces of equipment now in the Ministry of Works museum include two inscribed tags bearing the punched names of centurions, probably legionaries, so military occupation was not unexpected. A sequence of three or four auxiliary forts appears to have occupied the hill-top position, with pottery down to c. A.D. 75.[12] The earliest military occupation, however, is quite different in character, consisting of timber buildings which spread out to the south of the later forts and of Watling Street itself. No traces of any defences of this fort have been encountered, and its area could extend to the north, east and south for a considerable distance—only to the west does the ground drop away sharply. The pottery associated with these structures fits into the period c. A.D. 45–60. In view of the recent work at Wroxeter it would not be too improbable that we have here encountered the fortress of the XIVth Legion, moved into the forward area by Ostorius Scapula. Obviously a great deal more work is needed before this can be argued with conviction; there may be other surprises round the corner.

Proceeding west along Watling Street the next Roman site is the settlement at Pennocrucium. Apart from the civil site there are forts at Stretton Mill and Kinvaston, both discovered by Dr St Joseph. The first of these, on a small gravel plateau,[13] looks like a normal auxiliary fort of three-and-a-half acres; a more recent photograph taken by Mr Arnold Baker shows that it was preceded by a larger fort, as at Metchley. The fort at Kinvaston is much larger at twenty-six acres, enough for half a legion. The pottery, found by Dr St Joseph and in a later excavation,[14] fits into a context c. A.D. 60–70 rather than anything earlier, which must imply that this fort has nothing to do with the Scapulan advance, but rather with the troop

movements during the great revolt of Boudicca in A.D. 60.[15] However, there are further complications. Dr St Joseph now has evidence
that this fort was also later reduced, this time to eighteen acres,
presumably because troops were needed elsewhere. The next site
along Watling Street is at Red Hill, a height which overlooks the
Shropshire plain, and here again, straddling the road, is a small
enclosure which must mark the site of the settlement known as
Uxacona. On the higher ground is a sequence of military sites (*38*),
but the ditch systems are somewhat abnormal; they have not yet
been investigated and part of the site is now unfortunately occupied
by a reservoir.

On the north-west side of that dominating hog-back the Wrekin,
and by the side of the Severn, stood Viroconium, capital of the
Cornovii, one of the largest and most important towns of Roman
Britain. The evidence for its military origin consists of a series of
tombstones from a nearby cemetery of the following soldiers:[16]

1. Tiberius Claudius Terentius, a trooper of a Thracian cohort
2. Titus Flaminius, a soldier of the XIVth Legion
3. M. Petronius, a standard-bearer of the XIVth Legion
4. Valerius, a soldier probably of the XIVth Legion
5. Caius Mannius Secundus, of the XXth Legion

The presence of at least three stones of soldiers of the XIVth *Gemina*
clearly indicates that it was stationed at or near Wroxeter, but the
memorial of the man of the XXth does not at all imply that this
legion was here, as some have thought. This legionary is an old
soldier on the Governor's staff, and although he was on the strength
of the legion for pay and equipment, he would normally be serving
away from it on the business of the Governor (see Appendix IV).

Wroxeter, like the other sites, is beginning to produce complications. To date there are two small forts, three legionary fortresses
and two possible marching camps (*39*). The first sign of military
occupation was noticed by Dr St Joseph—a fort of five acres, 400
yards south of the town on the east bank of the Severn.[17] This fort
shows slight abnormalities in the ditch system which may reflect
more than one period with probably an earlier marching camp, but
the pottery found by Dr St Joseph in a trench and sherds picked up
on the surface are Claudian in date, although there is also some later

material. This may be the permanent auxiliary fort established by Ostorius Scapula after the advance to the Severn, and the unit could have been the Thracian cohort recorded on the tombstone of Terentius. Unfortunately the edge of that stone is damaged at the place where the number of the cohort would be given, but it may have been the VIth cohort, originally at Gloucester, which could have moved to these new quarters when the XXth Legion was established there. Another fort was found by Mr Arnold Baker in 1963, a mile north of the Roman city, on the Tern at Duncot. This is an unusually long and narrow shape, 230 feet by 820 feet, as if two auxiliary units had been placed side by side. The siting of this fort is on the main east–west line of advance, whereas the Roman city and the other fort are on the road leading towards the south-west and the Church Stretton gap. It almost seems as if the Duncot fort belongs to an early stage in the drive to the west, and this is confirmed by the presence of two marching camps nearby, one of which is on the disused Atcham airfield (37). A trench attempting to define the ditch of the latter ran into a deep gun-pit of the last war, an archaeological overlap which gives a gap in time of almost exactly 1,900 years. Neither site has yet produced any datable pottery; if the occupation was short, such evidence may be difficult to find.

Next we must consider the legionary fortresses, which have for some years been a problem that is only now being resolved. The Roman city lies on a sand and gravel plateau and much of its area produces very fine crop-marks of streets and buildings. There has in consequence been a good deal of aerial reconnaissance, specially directed towards finding military sites. It seems odd that after all this search no trace of a fifty-to-sixty-acre fortress has been found. Excavations in the city have produced a quantity of military equipment and Claudian coins, which seems to indicate that the fortress cannot be far away. In 1955 Dr St Joseph recorded two ditches, running under town buildings in the north-west sector and turning a well-formed corner,[18] and drew attention to their military character. But this ditch system was on alignment with the town street grid and Professor Sheppard Frere had already demonstrated something of the complexities of early town defences at Verulamium.[19] Caution seemed to be needed before arriving at conclusions. During the course of a training school which was conducted in 1958, a trench was cut across these ditches; but a spell of bad weather and a series of large rubbish pits of later date which had cut into the ditches prevented a section from being completed and studied in detail. It was clear, however, that the ditches were early in the history of the site and there were traces of a timber revetment on the inner lip. All this was hopeful but not conclusive. Meanwhile training schools had continued year by year from 1955 on the site of the baths; this was slow work, not planned as archaeological investigation, but as training for students in excavating technique. In the areas outside the massive stone structures of the bath-house whose foundations and basements had removed all the earlier levels, it soon became evident that there were timber buildings of the first century. These showed as trenches cut into the sand and back-filled with clean material. They were in fact the type of palisade trench used by the army to take the upright timbers on which the buildings were framed, as already described in the case of the fort at Waddon Hill in Dorset. But this was not immediately obvious, and there was the difficulty that these timber foundation works appeared eight feet below present ground level. If it had been possible to strip a large area to this depth the full significance of these early buildings would have been apparent sooner, but the method of working in square boxes was initiated for training students rather than solving archaeological problems; it was therefore some years before a large enough area had been excavated to demonstrate the nature of these buildings. Gradually it became evident that they were very large, with complex internal arrangements, and were very different from the simple type of strip-house usual in early civil development in Roman Britain. Furthermore, there seemed to be at least three periods of these buildings; in the final stage the whole had been demolished and the site levelled out prior to the erection of the first stone buildings on the site.[20] The historical implications of this need not concern us here since the pottery, of which there is now a fair quantity, is not earlier than c. A.D. 55–60. In other words, if, as now seems likely, we are in contact with the fortress of the XIVth Legion, it is evident that it was not established at Viroconium until that date. The only forts which should therefore concern us in the period of the initial advance are

39   *The Roman military sites at Wroxeter (Viroconium), Shropshire*

the auxiliary ones. Meanwhile, it seems as if the site of the fortress of the XIVth between *c.* A.D. 50 and 60 must be sought elsewhere. The evidence of pottery, as suggested above, inclines one at present towards Wall, undoubtedly a key site in these early years of the conquest.

The Severn must have been a major consideration in the strategy of the Ostorian campaign, but as yet very little evidence has been found of forts along its bank, apart from Gloucester and Wroxeter. Worcester is an obvious site and the number of British coins found here seem to postulate a pre-Roman river crossing. There was a Roman civil settlement here, whose name does not survive, and also of course an important Saxon, medieval and modern city. Unfortunately, with all the later occupation, there seems little hope of ever recovering much evidence of this early phase, but a ditch system of military pattern has been found south of the cathedral and King's School, which now stand on the site of the Norman castle. There is also evidence of a fort at Dodderhill near Droitwich, on the high ground overlooking the modern town. Small-scale excavations have produced Claudian pottery[21] and evidence of two periods of occupation, the second of which seems to be in the second century.[22] In the difficult country to the north, including the Ironbridge gap where there must surely be forts, there is so far nothing to report. The later fort near Cleobury Mortimer suggests a crossing of the Severn near Bewdley.

One of the most serious gaps at present is in the evidence of Roman military activity of this period beyond the Severn. Most of the archaeologists working in Wales seem to have assumed that the Roman occupation of the principality started in A.D. 75 with the governorship of Julius Frontinus. Yet, apart from the deep penetration that Scapula must have made in his campaigns, Tacitus says explicitly that he actually built forts in Silurian territory and was engaged in a bitter guerrilla warfare with the tribe at the time of his death. The only site which has produced any Claudian material west of the Severn is Usk, where there is sufficient from casual finds alone to postulate a fort of this period.[23] This could hardly have existed in splendid isolation; there must be other sites awaiting discovery. There is a remarkable twenty-five-acre fort at Clyro near Hay on the

Wye, occupying a key position for operations in this valley. The situation here, as in many of the midland forts, seems to be highly complicated, and only large-scale excavation will produce the full story. The siting and substantial defences of Clyro certainly make it a more permanent fort than has been previously suggested.[24]

Looking ahead, it is clear that the failure of Ostorius Scapula to bring the Silures to heel after the defeat of Caratacus made it necessary for him to maintain considerable forces in their territory; for to have retreated to the Severn and established his frontier on the east bank might have looked like defeat. The Roman Army seems thus to have been committed to maintaining a frontier in most difficult circumstances against an actively hostile population in hilly, forested terrain. Had it not been for the evidence from Usk one might be tempted to place an Ostorian frontier on the Wye, but it would seem more logical to postulate a defensive line from the Usk north through Monmouth to Kenchester (where several pieces of horse-trapping may indicate a military phase), Leintwardine and through the Church Stretton gap to Viroconium. But such an edifice cannot be created with only one brick. Although new military sites have been found and investigated along this line at Leintwardine, and to the rear at Wall Town near Cleobury Mortimer and elsewhere, in no case has any pre-Flavian material yet been found. Only the future holds the key to this series of problems concerning the last phase of Ostorius' operations in Wales.

III

The advance to the middle Severn brought much of the territory of the Cornovii under Roman control, and from bases on this new frontier it would be easy to strike at any of their malcontents still in arms. But the problems of the Deceangli remained, and the Roman commander must have been anxious to explore the territory between the Welsh hills and the south-western approaches to Brigantia, where military action might soon be needed. Perhaps he had in mind a Roman base in this area, to correspond to Lincoln in the east. The campaigning season of A.D. 49 was devoted to these objectives. Only one geographical detail is given for the attack on the Deceangli in this, the first Roman penetration into Wales. The concise account of Tacitus reads like many of the Welsh wars of English kings in the early Middle Ages. 'Their lands were ravaged, and booty was collected on all sides. The natives did not venture on a pitched battle, and when they did try to harass the column from ambush, their treachery was punished.' The Deceangli, it is clear, used sensible guerrilla tactics, whether at the instance of Caratacus or of their own leaders. The mention of lands laid waste gives some clue to the route taken by the Roman army, for the distribution of hill-forts makes it clear that some of the best lands of the Deceangli were in the Vale of Clwyd. How did the Romans reach them? The modern traveller approaching from the south-east enjoys the beautiful Vale of Llangollen and the spectacular road over the Horseshoe Pass; but this would be a dangerous approach for an invading army venturing into unknown territory. A more promising line would be up the valley of the River Alyn past Mold, then by Bodfari and the River Wheeler to the neighbourhood of Denbigh. A little further north, too, lies the route followed by the later Roman road, from Pentre Halkyn to the crossing of the Clwyd at St Asaph.

But Ostorius' problems were not confined to the Deceangli. 'They had almost reached the sea which looks towards Ireland, when trouble broke out among the Brigantes and forced the Roman general to retrace his steps. . . .' The point of return, perhaps, was somewhere near St Asaph or Rhuddlan. Intervention in Brigantia was now required. Here we may suspect the influence of Caratacus in the war-party of that nation, who became alarmed at the possibility of being outflanked, and cut off from Wales. 'The few who took up arms were killed, the rest were pardoned': again, Tacitus does not help to place events on the map. But the Romans presumably went as far as the upper Mersey, and one notes the hill-forts (Mam Tor, etc.) on the western slopes of the Peak. The northern Camulodunum (Almondbury, near Huddersfield) was an important political centre: it is just possible that the Roman army penetrated so far in support of Queen Cartimandua. Certainly Tacitus here implies both military action and a political settlement. By the time these were concluded, the season for campaigning was over and the Roman units were withdrawn to base.

It would be quite possible for Ostorius to present the year's work in a favourable light, and his attempt to do so seems to have been the source for Tacitus. Yet his objectives (if we have defined them correctly) were largely unattained. He had now learned something of the topography of north-east Wales, and of the problems of coming to closer grips with the Brigantes. But the Roman frontier remained as it had been, and the fighting strength of the Deceangli was unimpaired and able to stand again with Caratacus another year.

IV

At this point a reappraisal must have been forced on the Roman Governor. After two years of office, the problems ahead of him were far more formidable than any he had yet solved. The policy of dealing with the tribes individually, applying *clementia* or *atrocitas* as the case demanded, had failed: thanks to Caratacus, there was a cohesion among them for which he had not allowed. Above all, there was the hostility of the Silures. The most warlike and the most powerful of the Welsh tribes, neither diplomacy nor force had as yet the slightest effect on them. Operations must already have been undertaken in the difficult country between the Severn and the Wye, and will have shown that it was impossible to control them from the auxiliary forts established by Aulus Plautius along the lower Severn. A major campaign must now be undertaken in South Wales, and the main strength of the legions be brought to bear on the Silures. More was involved in this deployment than a simple march to the west. Discontent was still alive in the eastern part of the province, and it would not do to leave it stripped of forces.

Against this background, Ostorius' decision to found a military colony at Camulodunum is seen as the logical application of a well-tried policy. It had been a legionary base since A.D. 43. The legions had now been in Britain for six years, and it may be assumed that— had there been no discharges—between a quarter and a third of the men were now due for retirement. Their land-grants could come from the estates of the royal house of Cunobelinus: Camulodunum was famous throughout the island, and easily reached from the continent. Here, too, the eleven British kings had surrendered to

Claudius in A.D. 43. No other place seemed so suitable for the capital of the province, the centre of the cult of Claudius, and the show-piece of civilisation. The strong force of veterans (perhaps two or three thousand men?), established here by Ostorius on a new site close to the old native capital in the winter of 49–50, had a double purpose to discharge. A reserve to be used in case of trouble, they were also expected, with the example of their unswerving loyalty to Rome, 'to instruct the friendly natives in the duties enjoined by the laws'. In view of the history of the colony, Tacitus' words have an ironic ring. For the overbearing arrogance and greed of the veterans of Camulodunum did more than anything else to induce the Trinovantes to join the tribal cause under Boudicca only eleven years later (A.D. 60). It is an altogether different story from that of Cologne, made a colony in A.D. 50,[25] where Roman soldiers and the German tribe of the Ubii had, by 69, come to regard themselves as a single community, whose sympathies in the rebellion of Civilis were unswervingly with Rome. Not much can be said for the veterans of Camulodunum, who showed Roman imperialism in the worst light. But perhaps it should be remembered that these same men, six years earlier, had regarded an expedition to Britain as taking them beyond the limits of the known world. It cannot have pleased them to know that they were now expected to live there for the rest of their lives.

V

The winter of 49–50 must have been a busy one for Ostorius, with the affairs of the *colonia* to supervise, as well as all the preparations for the most serious campaigns in Britain since the invasion itself. At last all was ready. *Itum inde in Siluras*. Early in the summer of A.D. 50, the XXth Legion, in the full panoply of a Roman army marching out for battle, left its base at Gloucester to cross the Severn and advance towards the hills of South Wales. Yet another force will have left Viroconium, to probe up the Severn valley towards Caersws, and to stop reinforcements reaching Caratacus from the north. But Ostorius was not to lay his foe by the heels that summer. The Roman forces were operating in difficult country and against a wily opponent—the first general in history, it would seem, to view the military problems of Wales as a whole. If actions were fought, Tacitus does not mention them. Caratacus had plenty of room to manœuvre, and it would suit him well to let the Romans exhaust themselves in long marches while he was continually threatening an engagement but always slipping away. Ostorius, too, may have been content simply to get to know the routes into the mountains and round their flanks, to explore the river valleys and to select sites for a network of forts that would ensure a permanent Roman hold on the country. Doubtless booty was taken wherever possible and settlements burned to discourage the people from lending help to the enemy. Marching camps are known in the Ludlow gap at Bromfield and Upper Affcot, also in Glamorgan on Silurian territory.[26] None of them can be dated, at present, but some may well belong to these operations. Perhaps, too, a column will have advanced down the western bank of the Severn to Chepstow, where a discerning eye could have noted its unsuitability as a supply base because of the great range of the tides.

Coupled with these probes into the Welsh Marches would have been extensive naval patrols. Operating from the Bristol Channel and the north coast of Devon, the squadron sweeping along the southern Welsh shore must have perturbed the Silures with the prospect of a sea-borne invasion while their main fighting strength was elsewhere.[27] No protection could be offered on the water and the galleys paraded up and down: the precise rhythm of their oars gave the shore watchers cause for alarm. There are two small signal-stations on the coast of Devon, at Old Burrow and Martinhoe. Excavations have shown that the first of these could well belong to this period, with coins of Tiberius and Claudius and a military entrenching tool. Martinhoe has produced coins of Nero (A.D. 64–8) and either continued in use or belongs to a later occasion.[28] It is also possible, as Dr Michael Jarrett has reminded us, that the fleet was used to promote land operations much further to the west. The Towy offers a line of penetration to the west of the Silures, and the traces of pre-Flavian occupation in the forts at Neath and Llandovery prompt one to ask whether it was exploited by Ostorius.

Little military glory was won by the Roman Army that summer, but at the end of it Ostorius probably felt that he had learned enough about the country of the Silures to turn it into a trap for Caratacus. Another season the trap could be sprung.

Caratacus, who will have made his own appraisal, seems to have reached the same conclusion. Ostensibly, he had done well to keep Roman power at bay for a further year, but the performance could hardly be repeated. Perhaps, too, there were growing tensions in his relations with the tribes of Wales, at which we can only guess. His policy meant virtually the maintenance of a standing army, something alien to the Celtic traditions of warfare. There were compensations so long as booty could be had by raiding the Roman province, but the new frontier defences of Ostorius ruled that out. The economic burden of maintaining Caratacus' own force must have been considerable. Henceforward, there was the prospect of a war each summer on Welsh soil—and the Deceangli and the Silures could testify what that would mean. *Atrocitas* was beginning to pay dividends. The position of a war-leader in a confederacy of Celtic peoples was precarious: success was an essential ingredient. There could have been many grumbles against Caratacus that winter among the tribal chieftains of Wales. Considerations such as these forced the British general to seize the initiative for the campaign of A.D. 51, and to fight on new ground and with a new strategy. In Tacitus' account,[29] there is a justifiable note of surprise: 'Next Caratacus, inferior to us in numbers, but superior in cunning and knowledge of the country, transferred the fighting to the country of the Ordovices. Joined by all who feared the "*pax Romana*", he determined to stake everything on a pitched battle. He had chosen a site where the approach routes, lines of retreat, and all other factors were to his advantage and our disadvantage. . . .'

Before discussing the vexed question of where this place of strength may be, it is necessary to try to understand the hopes on which Caratacus' new policy was based. The move to the land of the Ordovices, from south-east to central and northern Wales, is obvious enough. It avoids encirclement on the Black Mountains by a Roman thrust up the Wye and the Usk. It keeps open the lines of communication with Brigantia, for reinforcements as well as for retreat—hence the presence of those who 'feared the Roman peace'. But the decison to choose a strong place to stand and fight is different: it is not thus that inferior forces can usually hope to win a Welsh campaign. Caratacus must have foreseen no future for himself in Wales unless he could win a decisive victory. And history afforded grounds for such hope—the same grounds that had prompted resistance to the invasion of A.D. 43. If a strong enough position could be found, the Romans might be led on to disaster, and then there would be a free Wales at least. And if he lost, the struggle could be renewed in Brigantia. So once more the tribal levies gathered round Caratacus and the Belgic war-band he had brought to Wales. We do not know how numerous were the dissidents who rallied to him from Brigantia and from within the province, but he must have headed a formidable body of fighting men, hating the Roman invader and convinced that their cause was just.

In the fighting of 51, Ostorius had to play a hand where the cards had been dealt by Caratacus. How long it took him to discover the chosen redoubt, whether there was any preliminary skirmishing, whether he waited for his forces to unite or used the northern column alone for the final battle, we do not know. Tacitus, with his instinct for the dramatic, hurries on to describe the Roman forces halted in front of a river whose fords are unknown. Beyond it the hills rise steeply, their slopes bristling with armed men. So we reach that famous site which, as Haverfield complains, 'the imagination of local antiquaries has placed on every hill-top in the Border'. Such imaginations were too seldom controlled by a close study of the words of Tacitus: 'a site where the approach routes, lines of retreat, and all other factors were to his advantage and our disadvantage. On the one side were steep hills, and where they did offer an easier line of ascent they had piled boulders to form a rampart. A river flowed in front of the position, and its fords had not been tested, while bands of armed warriors lined the defences.' Further, the account of the battle makes it clear that the steep slopes rose to a summit plateau, while the escape of Caratacus suggests a place not easily surrounded, and with good lines of escape to the north and north-east. To summarise—a complex group of hills, rising above a large river, with a summit plateau, in the land of the Ordovices— these are the conditions which any candidate for the position is required to satisfy. Reflection will suggest other negative indications.

It is not a hill-fort of the ordinary kind—the defences have had to be improvised. It is hardly likely to be in the mountains of Snowdonia—Caratacus will not go so far north-west lest he be cornered and cut off from Brigantia. Nor is it anywhere in north-east Wales, for that is the land of the Deceangli. Somewhere then, in north-central Wales: and if so, there would seem to be only two suitable rivers, the upper Severn and the Dee. No site along the Dee impresses us, but there are two on the Severn whose claims we rank high.

The first of these, Cefncarnedd, has a long-standing local tradition, now revived by the distinguished support of Dr J. K. St Joseph.[30] It forms part of a line of hills between Caersws and Llanidloes, rising on a front of rather more than four miles to the west of the Severn, with the valley of the Tarannog and its tributaries on the opposite side. Cefncarnedd (908 feet) itself is the northernmost point of the group which reaches a height of 1,007 feet at Gelli Hir. Dr St Joseph rightly draws attention to the strategic importance of this site at the junction of routes to South Wales, the Shropshire plain, and Cardigan Bay. The Roman fort at Caersws, and the railway junction at Moat Lane, were founded to take advantage of this nodal point of communications in Wales. He points out how admirably this great natural amphitheatre would serve as the focus of the southernmost sept of the Ordovices. It would, indeed, and such no doubt was the function of the hill-fort which has given its name to Cefncarnedd. But a close inspection shows these hills at a disadvantage as the site of Caratacus' redoubt. As seen from Llandinam, Cefncarnedd does not rise very steeply above the river, and there is flat land on either side which could contain large Roman forces before and after the crossings. Moreover, Cefncarnedd itself is cut off from the rest of the group by an easy pass, now followed by the minor road from Llandinam to Trewythen. Further south, the Wigdwr Brook gives another easy line of penetration. The position, in fact, could be easily surrounded and the cavalry patrols would be lax indeed to allow Caratacus to escape.

We would therefore draw attention to another site some three miles to the east of Newtown, just opposite Abermule. Here, on a front of rather more than a mile, between Dolforwyn Hall and

Aberbechan, the hills rise very steeply from the north bank of the Severn to about 800 feet. The strategic importance of this site is marked by Dolforwyn Castle: it must be conceded there is no sign or tradition whatsoever of any Roman or pre-Roman antiquities. But—and this is the point—once the plateau by Dolforwyn Castle is gained, a tangled mass of hilly country, nowhere much above 1,000 feet but deeply dissected by streams, is seen stretching northwards for some ten miles to the valley of the Vyrnwy to the east of Llanfair Caereinion. Such country could not be easily patrolled, and, once the Vyrnwy is reached, the broad Vale of Meifod leads north-east to the Shropshire plain, the Dee and the Mersey. We present these two places on a short-list, without venturing a final choice. Archaeology may one day decide between them, or produce a better candidate.

VI

For the battle that followed, Tacitus is the only guide. His description[31] is one of the best of the four surviving British battle scenes, and is marked by the speed and concinnity of his mature powers. Such literary set-pieces are especially designed for the reader's pleasure: it may be that some of their flavour will survive translation.

> The British chieftains went round their tribal levies, making light of their fears, encouraging their hopes, and offering other incentives to arms. Caratacus hastened from one point to the next, proclaiming that this was the day and this the battle which would either win back their freedom, or mark the beginning of eternal slavery. He called on the names of their ancestors, who had put to flight the dictator Julius Caesar; it was through their valour that they lived free from the lictor's axe and the tax-collector's demands, and that the bodies of their wives and children were undefiled. These words were greeted with applause, and every man bound himself, with the oath of his people, never to yield to weapons or wounds. Their spirit dismayed the Roman commander, as did the river between the armies, the strengthened defences, the overhanging ridges, and the fierce warriors who crowded every point. All made up a black picture. But the soldiers demanded battle, saying that valour could carry any position: their officers spoke in the same way and encouraged them still further. Then Ostorius made a reconnaissance to determine which points would yield and which would not, and led forward his eager troops.

The river-crossing offered no obstacle. When they reached the embankment, there was a sharp exchange of missiles, with more deaths and casualties on the Roman side. But then they locked shields to form a 'tortoise', hurled down the rudely-built rampart, and brought about a hand-to-hand battle on equal terms. The barbarians retreated to the hill-top, but here too our men followed them, the light-armed auxiliaries using their spears, the legionaries in close order. The British ranks were thrown into confusion, for they had no protection from breast-plate or helmets: if they made a stand against the auxiliaries, they were mown down by the swords and spears of the legionaries, if they turned against the latter, they met the long swords and pikes of the auxiliaries. It was a glorious victory: the wife and daughter of Caratacus were captured, and his brothers surrendered. He himself fled to Cartimandua, Queen of the Brigantes. But there is no refuge in adversity, and he was bound in chains and handed over to us. This was the ninth year of the war in Britain.

The passage is masterly in its selection of significant detail—the nature of the country, the feelings of the contestants, the issues at stake for the Britons, the successive phases of the battle, and the technical superiority by which victory was won. Like the scenes on Trajan's Column—almost contemporary with the *Annals*—it gives the essence of a battle, as recorded by a great artist. So, at Stratford, the words of Shakespeare, the skill of producer and actor, and the dreadful ringing of steel on steel, conveyed the essence of the Wars of the Roses. But questions are now in order, and modern accounts of battles call for more details than these. First, what were the numbers engaged on both sides? The statement that the Roman general had the larger forces refers presumably to the campaign as a whole rather than to this battle. Two legions with auxiliaries would give Ostorius Scapula some 20,000 troops deployed in Wales, of whom perhaps between 12,000 and 15,000 might have taken part in the last battle. The army of Caratacus, then, is not likely to have exceeded 10,000 men. This was a confederate army, made up of tribal contingents. How many, and from which tribes? The description suggest at least three, possibly more. The Silures, Ordovices and Deceangli are certain contributors, perhaps the Demetae, and a rebel force from the Brigantes in addition to Caratacus' own Belgae. In all, some five contingents at least, each fighting under its own leaders. The rebellion of Civilis in Gaul (A.D. 70) offers parallels on a larger scale. At the siege of Vetera the Batavians and the German tribes were posted 'each tribe by itself, so that in isolation the valour of each could be more clearly seen'. At the same site but in the later battle which was to decide the issue of the rebellion, Civilis was in command of a contingent from the Batavi, the Cugerni, and two or more German tribes.[32] Such heterogeneous barbarian armies must have presented problems of command which Roman generals were spared. A contest of valour might be useful, if the day went well: in adversity each group would be only too likely to look after itself. No wonder that the Britons were called upon to swear, 'each man by the oath of his tribe', to resist to the end. Such tribal oaths, incidentally, are familiar in the battles in the hero-tales of Ireland. And in other respects, too, Tacitus has caught the spirit of a great Celtic host. The fierce appearance of the warriors and their wild costumes, the clash of arms and the raucous blast of the *carnyx*, the Celtic trumpet, the impassioned appeal of the chieftains—all this sound and fury could shake even experienced Roman troops. One senses, too, that an ingredient in the *atrox spectaculum* which disconcerted Ostorius and his men was the day itself. One of those lowering days, perhaps, too common in a Welsh summer, when the clouds hang low and black, and the mountains look higher and steeper than they really are. But, as the soldiers said, courage would carry the day. A battle now, they probably felt, would be better than more footslogging round the hills of Wales in the rain.

The engagement itself falls into three clearly defined phases. First, the river-crossing. Once the fords had been found, this proved easier than expected: here it may be said that there are four fords in little more than a mile in front of the Dolforwyn position. It does not seem to have been a contested crossing—though harassed by missiles no doubt—for the Britons were reserving their main efforts for resistance at the rock-barriers. With cover, and the advantage of the slope, they were able to inflict sizeable losses at these points, but the *testudo* formation proved its value once again. Caratacus, unlike some of the tribes beyond the Rhine frontier, had not had much practice in the art of fortification. Driven from their defences to the summit-plateau, the Britons felt in full measure the Roman superiority in weapons and armour. The short, rigid stabbing sword of the legionary always had a deadly margin over the long cutting sword of the Celt: but now, too, the specialised weapons of the auxiliaries came into play. Only the British chieftains wore helmets and armour—the common soldiers had to go into action almost naked—indeed, they may have preferred it, as Highland troops have sometimes done even in modern times. In tribal warfare this would not matter, but against a Roman army they were placed at a fatal disadvantage. It was at this point that the British ranks gave way, and the day was lost. So far the battle had followed the classic pattern for engagements between Roman and Celtic forces. But there was usually a final phase that is here absent—pursuit and slaughter. No British casualty figures are given for this battle, in contrast to the 10,000 claimed at Mons Graupius, or 80,000 for Suetonius' victory over Boudicca.[33] Now pursuit and slaughter is the task of the cavalry, and there is no mention of Roman cavalry—nor of British chariots—in Tacitus' account. Clearly the battle was fought over country where cavalry was useless or could operate only with difficulty—another pointer to Caratacus' skilled choice of ground. It is worth comparing this battle with the similar action fought by Petilius Cerialis against the rebellious Treveri under Valentinus.[34] This took place at Rigodulum (Riol), a strong position in the Moselle Valley between Trier and Bingen. The hill of Rigodulum is much higher than either of our sites in the upper Severn, and the Moselle is a larger river: there, too, the enemy occupied the position in force, and had built defensive works at weak points. But Cerialis was able to use his cavalry in the frontal assault on the hill: more important still, another force worked its way round over easier ground, and coming from the Hunsruck took the Treveri in the rear, 'capturing Valentinus and the Belgic chiefs'. Such a catch did not fall to Ostorius. Caratacus' brothers surrendered, no doubt in the course of the fighting. His wife and daughter were captured—by what mischance we do not know. But Caratacus escaped again, as he did from the battle at the Medway, and it is likely that horses hidden on the flatter ground of the plateau will have carried him, with a small force of bodyguard, out of reach of any Roman pursuit. Others too seem to have got safely away. Only a few months later the Silures are found fighting with undaunted ferocity 'to avenge the defeat of so great a king'. The inference is clear—the action on the Severn made no heavy inroads on their fighting strength, nor perhaps on that of the other Welsh tribes. Caratacus will have given the order to disperse before he made his own escape.

For Ostorius, of course, it was indeed a famous victory, and it had shattered the British confederacy. But it is clear that Caratacus did not think it the end of the war. That this is so follows from the course he now took—escape to Brigantia. Tacitus pictures this as the action of a desperate fugitive who throws himself on the mercy of Cartimandua, only to be betrayed by her and delivered up to the Romans. There are good grounds for mistrusting this assessment. If all Caratacus wanted was a bolt-hole, there were not lacking in Wales places where he and a few friends could have maintained themselves, even for years, as Owen Glyndwr did after the battle of Shrewsbury. The Snowdon massif, for example, where he would have the support of the Ordovices and the Druids. Or the lonely wilderness of Plynlimmon, or the steep green mountains and deep cwms of Mawddwy, from which in the mid-sixteenth century the Gwylliaid Cochion or Red Banditti terrorised the countryside for years, defying all attempts to round them up. Had he felt, like Commius, King of the Atrebates, that he would go where he would never look on a Roman again, he could have fled to Ireland. That he rejected these possibilities in favour of Brigantia makes his purpose clear—the renewal of the war. The long-term prospects for such a course would have seemed promising. The Brigantes were a powerful and warlike people, and though the anti-Roman party was in eclipse for the moment, with his help it could perhaps gain the ascendancy. If so, the Pennines would be the ideal country for the British resistance: better than Wales, because behind them lay the man-power and fastnesses of Caledonia. The Silures were still in the field, and, if contact with Wales could be kept, it might be possible to concert an attack against the province on two fronts. Caratacus could still offer a threat to Rome. But the immediate hazards were obvious. Chief among them was the position of Cartimandua. He would depend on her sympathy, initially, though no doubt the diplomatic spadework had already been done to renew in the north his powers as war-leader. After all, when he fled to Wales he had been in just this situation.

It is at this point that Queen Cartimandua, whose political and amorous adventures were to play so large a part in the history of Britain for the next eighteen years, is first mentioned by name in the historical narrative of Tacitus, as we have it. Had his account of the Claudian invasion survived, we should know whether—as seems almost certain—she was indeed the ruler of the Brigantes when that state first became a client-kingdom. The heiress of a royal house whose male line was extinct, she sat on an uneasy throne. Geography and politics alike made for centrifugal tendencies among the Brigantes. Links between the royal line and that of Cunobelinus have been suspected, but not proved; archaeology discloses cultural ties with the Druids of Mona and the tribes of north-east Wales and its borders.

Caratacus cannot have come as a stranger to the Queen of the Brigantes, but his presence must have seemed full of menace. She ruled over a faction-ridden state with the support of Rome. Without it, perhaps, she would have lost her throne, as she so nearly did eighteen years later. Her enemies were the enemies of Rome: to shelter Caratacus would be to help them to power. To what ties of kinship or patriotism or religion Caratacus appealed we do not know. He spoke to deaf ears. And when a Roman mission appeared to demand his surrender, it was in the logic of the situation that she should comply. Caratacus in chains—what greater service could she render to Rome? For not merely did it seem to put an end to the war in Britain, but it was most useful to official propaganda. The prestige of Claudius' regime had been badly shaken by the excesses of the freedmen and the scandals of Messalina, culminating in her death in A.D. 47. The new Empress, Agrippina, was anxious to promote great State ceremonies at which she could appear as consort: Claudius himself had a taste for such occasions, whether from policy or private inclination. The capture of Caratacus could be made to recall the glorious days of A.D. 44—and not only in Rome. Tacitus leaves no doubt that Caratacus with his family and retinue appeared in a series of public displays virtually all the way from Britain to the capital. 'His fame had spread beyond the British islands, had penetrated the western provinces, and was well-known in Italy itself. All were eager to see the man who had so long defied Roman power.' Of the details of this journey we know nothing and can only imagine its effects on Caratacus' mind. As he passed through the northern parts of Gaul he would have seen the growing prosperity of a land that had learned to accept the Roman rule. Then followed, perhaps, the splendour of Lugdunum and the cities of Gallia Narbonensis. Did he see the triumphal arch at Arausio (Orange) in honour of Caesar's victories, and realise that the man 'defeated by my ancestors' had some solid and permanent achievements to his credit in Celtic lands? All this is conjecture. But that the magnificence and power of Roman civilisation impressed him deeply is clear from what he said in Rome.

VII

The surrender of Caratacus was regarded, so Tacitus says, as an embellishment of the triumph of Claudius. It was also thought (wrongly) to mark the end of the fighting in Wales, and indeed in Britain, for the arrangement with the client kingdom of the Brigantes had held firm under stress. With the surrender of the last of Cunobelinus' sons, Claudius' objectives in Britain could be taken as attained. There could hardly be another triumph, but the occasion was marked by a grand military review and a special session of the Senate.

The review was held on the parade-ground of the Praetorian Guard, with the city cohorts under arms, and the Roman people looking on. Claudius sat on a tribunal with Agrippina at his side; a novelty which drew unfavourable comment from Tacitus, but another sign of the importance accorded to the Empress and to the Imperial House.[35] There was a parade of captives, as in a triumph. 'As the King's followers marched along, their decorations and torcs and the spoils they had won in wars against the other British tribes were displayed. Then came Caratacus' brothers, his wife and daughter, finally the King himself. . . .' There follows the famous speech of Caratacus:

> Had my high birth and rank been accompanied by moderation in the hour of success, I should have entered this city as a friend and not a prisoner. You would not have hesitated to accept as an ally a man of splendid ancestry, bearing rule over many tribes. My present position

is degrading to me, but glorious to you. I had horses, warriors, and gold: if I was unwilling to lose them, what wonder in that? Does it follow that, because you desire universal empire, all must accept universal slavery? Were I now dragged here as one who had surrendered without fighting, no fame would have attached to my fall nor to your victory. If you punish me they will both be forgotten. Spare me, then, to be an eternal example of your mercy!

Short as it is, it must rank with the best of Tacitean speeches. But is it more than a rhetorical composition? Can it be used by the historian of Roman Britain? Now while Tacitus does not claim to reproduce the works of a speaker, he uses speeches to throw light on the motives of the speaker and the facts of the situation. This ceremony was obviously carefully stage-managed, and needed a speech from Caratacus as its climax. And there is evidence, apart from Tacitus, to show that he did speak and that what he said was remembered. Zonaras, following Dio Cassius, records his comment on Roman magnificence. 'And when you have all this, do you still envy us our hovels?'[36] Granted that we may use Caratacus' speech in the *Annals* as evidence, there are three things to be noted. First, a suggestion that he once had the chance of coming to terms with Rome, but turned it down. The words, with a suggestion of an offer of client kingship, fit best into the context of the diplomatic offensive earlier alluded to (p. 49). The second is his steady belief in the value of *libertas*, in defiance of all the aims of Roman imperialism. And the third—his appeal to the *clementia* or mercy of the Emperor.

This last is the real point of the speech, and is underlined by what was said in the 'long and extravagant speeches' in the special session of the Senate. The surrender of Caratacus was compared to the display of Syphax by Scipio Africanus, of Perseus by Aemilius Paullus. The senators knew their Roman history and they had taken the point. Tacitus conceals it. For Syphax and Perseus were not only kings exhibited at the most glorious triumphs of the old Republic. They were also outstanding examples of the mutability of human affairs, moving their noble Roman conquerors to compassion, and causing them to reflect on the need for moderation and clemency. When Syphax was brought into the Roman camp 'even Scipio was moved by the contrast between his former prosperity and his present lot . . .'.[37] Still more striking was the case of Perseus, a greater king and of a more famous race, as told by Livy and, on a more ample scale, by Plutarch. Paullus rose to meet Perseus, shedding tears, as he was brought into his headquarters. But Perseus abased himself with shameful entreaties (unlike Caratacus!), and met the stern reproach that courage in misfortune brings praise even from enemies, but that the Romans consider cowardice, even if successful, the most disgraceful of qualities. Then Paullus spoke of fortune and of human affairs, and called on the young men of his staff to abandon empty insolence and the pride of victory. Livy also relates how Paullus tried to comfort Perseus with the thought that 'the clemency of the Roman people, proven in the disasters of so many kings and peoples, offers you not merely a hope but almost a firm guarantee of safety'. For Caratacus, of course, it was *clementia principis* and not *clementia populi Romani*; but it was subtle on the part of the Senate to set Claudius side by side with the high-souled heroes of the Republic. No compliment could have been more acceptable to an Emperor with his veneration for the Roman past, himself the pupil of Livy.

How the eight years of operations in Britain were made use of by official propaganda will now be clear. In words that we have used elsewhere: 'A Roman expedition, well-officered and brilliantly led, crosses the Ocean and lands in Britain, smashing barriers which we have called both geographical and psychological. When the Emperor takes the field in person, the most powerful state in Britain is quickly defeated. The resistance of other British states is usually short-lived, though sharp in the south-west. A British province takes shape, buttressed by client kingdoms whose loyalty stands up under stress. Only in Wales, under Caratacus, is resistance prolonged. When at last that prince is overcome, there is a notable display of Imperial *clementia* to a gallant adversary. The recklessness of Caesar, the fiasco of Gaius, are not repeated. There is a break with the inertia of Tiberius. Throughout the model is Augustus. The bounds of the Empire are extended to the western limit of the known world, and the sacred *pomoerium* of Rome enlarged by an Emperor whose *pietas* has once again placed her in the right relationship with the gods.'

Wars against the Silures and the Brigantes

A.D. 51–57

6

The impressive picture built up by Roman propaganda had a serious flaw. It was not accepted in the lands west of the Severn. The Silures were unappeased and unsubdued. Stung by the loss of Caratacus, they took the field again, and 'as if to avenge the death of so great a king', waged a relentless and brilliant guerrilla warfare that brought Ostorius Scapula to his grave. His successor, Didius Gallus, made no advances in Wales, and was faced with troubles in Brigantia, for which he achieved only a temporary solution. The last phase of the Claudian Conquest of Britain is thus marked by setbacks and loss of momentum. These produced a disillusion with the whole British venture so acute that, early in the reign of Nero, serious consideration was given to abandoning the new province. Not until A.D. 57 was a decision made to go forward, and it implies a throwing overboard of the Claudian policy of limited conquest in the lowland zone of Britain for a new design involving the conquest of Wales. Events in Britain and elsewhere were to postpone its realisation for a further twenty years. Quintus Veranius, the governor appointed to put the Neronian forward policy into operation, died in his first year of office. His successor, Suetonius Paulinus, was on the point of completing the conquest of North Wales when the great rebellion led by Boudicca (A.D. 60) broke out in his rear, and the province was almost lost. The governors who had to deal with its aftermath were compelled to think in terms of reconstruction and reform, rather than of conquest. Then came the civil wars of A.D. 69. Not until Vespasian was firmly in control could Rome produce splendid armies and great generals, Petilius Cerealis, Julius Frontinus, and Julius Agricola, who would lead them forward once more into the highland zone, and attempt the conquest of Caledonia.

It is worth looking ahead to see the whole pattern of events to follow. But our concern here is with the first five years only, A.D. 52–7, and with the work of the last two governors appointed by Claudius. Once again, we are wholly dependent on Tacitus, and for a story which he does not choose to tell at length. The campaigns of these years were indecisive, devoid of incidents gratifying to Roman pride, like the last stand of Caratacus. Didius Gallus, elderly and disinclined for further exertion, belongs to that class of governor of Britain whom Tacitus regarded with contempt. Yet we can discern in his narrative,[1] for all its compression, events as dramatic as any we have yet encountered, and marked with the added interest of British success.

The renewal of hostilities by the Silures clearly took by surprise the Roman army and its high command. Ostorius had supposed that their fighting spirit was broken by the defeat of Caratacus, and that he could now keep them under control by building a network of forts in their territory. A substantial number of legionary cohorts were detailed for these duties, protected by auxiliary units; the rest of the legion's forces were presumably withdrawn to their bases at Gloucester and (perhaps) Wall. The first sign of trouble was an attack on the temporary camp of one of these construction parties, under the command of a *praefectus castrorum*. The Silurian force was large enough to have carried the Roman position and massacred its defenders, but messengers had got through to the nearest forts and help arrived in the nick of time. As it was, the commanding officer, eight centurions, and, to use Tacitus' words, 'the bravest fighters from the ranks' were killed—a striking success for the Silures. It was soon followed by another action, which might well rank among the most important battles of the whole Claudian invasion if a full account of it had been given by Tacitus. It began with a Silurian attack on a Roman foraging party, which was put to flight, along with cavalry squadrons sent to their support. Ostorius himself now took a hand, sending in infantry reinforcements. These, too, failed to check the Roman rout, and the main strength of at least two legions had to be flung in. First the position was stabilised, then the Roman got the upper hand: but by now the day was far advanced and the enemy (significant phrase!) 'got away with only slight loss'. Encouraged by their success, the Silures now passed over to a

40   *The Roman road between Craven Arms and Leintwardine,*
which probably marked the frontier of Ostorius Scapula

41 *Roman cavalry equipment, from the Seven Sisters Hoard, Glamorgan (See Appendix VI, p. 194)*

general offensive. This next phase was marked by frequent engagements and—perhaps even more telling—by widespread guerrilla
warfare, vividly described by Tacitus. 'More often they crept
through the glens and swamps like bandits—each man as chance
offered or courage led, accidentally or deliberately, for booty or for
revenge, at the command of their leaders—or sometimes, without
their knowledge.'

No place names are given for any of the events described above,
except that the first action took place 'in the territory of the Silures',
as presumably did all the others. The modern reader will hardly be
content if no effort is made to place them on the map. Clyro, one may
suggest, could very well be the scene of the first action. To control
the Silures it would be essential to hold the Wye Valley, and this
large fort, now believed to contain traces of Claudian occupation,[2]
is, in size and position, most suitable as the base for a large construction party sent out from Gloucester under a camp commandant.
It is less easy to suggest the 'nearest forts' from which help was sent.
The fort at Usk would be thirty-five miles away, Llandovery about
the same, Neath nearly fifty miles. These distances seem too large
for help to arrive quickly. There may, of course, have been other
forts on the Black Mountain fringes, built in the earlier campaigns
against Caratacus, whose sites we do not know.[3] For the second and
bigger action, a clue would be provided if we could be sure that it
took place within half a day's march of a main legionary base. This
could only be at Gloucester. But it is more likely that by now
Ostorius was in the field at the head of an expeditionary force: the
mention of two legions is strong support for this view. The 'glens
and swamps' of the guerrilla phase could well be the wooded hills
of the Forest of Dean and the marshes of the lower Severn, through
which raiding parties of the Silures could find their way into the
Roman province.

Tacitus, however, is usually more interested in the mood of the
combatants than the place of the action. He leaves us in no doubt of
Ostorius' feelings at this juncture—they were that mixture of exas-
peration and fury which seems in all ages an occupational hazard of
the high command. A year ago he had been voted triumphal honours
for a war that he was supposed to have won: now he looked like

losing it. The military situation was alarming: worse still, he was made to look ridiculous. Tacitus has a sarcastic comment on the premature triumphal honours decreed to supposed conquerors of the Numidian chief Tacfarinas in the reign of Tiberius—'there were already three laurelled statues in Rome, yet Tacfarinas was still plundering Africa'.[4] Remarks of this kind may have been let fall incautiously over the wine in mess at Gloucester. It is under such circumstances that a general's mind will turn to thoughts of extermination, and so it was with Ostorius. 'The very name of the Silures', he declared, 'must be completely wiped out, as happened to the Sugambri, who were either massacred or transported to Gaul!'[5]

The choice of example is illuminating, for it recalls a notable piece of Roman ruthlessness (*atrocitas*) in dealing with a barbarian people. The Sugambri, a hostile people living on the east bank of the Rhine, had, in the reign of Augustus, first to suffer a reduction of their fighting strength in their own lands, and were then transported into Gallia Belgica, where they lost their tribal identity. Their men were taken away to fight as auxiliaries in the Roman army: although the name Sugambri continues to appear on military inscriptions down to the second century A.D., it signifies little more than the name of the unit. As a political entity, the Sugambri had ceased to exist. It was a ruthless solution—as ruthless as anything applied in modern times to the American Indian. The general's purpose became known to the Silures—through prisoners, deserters, or spies?—and, not surprisingly, did nothing to diminish the 'peculiar stubbornness' (*praecipua pervicacia*) of that people.[6]

In the grimmer phase that had now developed it was the Silures who struck the next blow. Two Roman auxiliary units, engaged on ravaging their territory, failed to take the precautions needed against so bold and nimble an enemy. They were surrounded, and either killed or taken prisoner. It is tempting to read Tacitus' *incautius* in a geographical sense, and to suppose that they had gone too far into enemy territory, beyond the range of Roman support which saved the situation in our two earlier instances—a penetration, perhaps, into the Plain of Gwent? The defeated Romans were more useful alive than dead, for we are told that 'by distributing among them spoils and prisoners the Silures were inciting other British tribes to rebellion' (*ceteras quoque nationes ad defectionem trahebant*). The word *defectio*, if taken strictly, would suggest tribes within the Roman province—unless some sort of agreement had been reached with the other three tribes of Wales after the defeat of Caratacus. In any case, it is clear that the successes of the Silures had encouraged anti-Roman elements everywhere, and that a new and formidable native confederacy was taking shape.

Atrocitas might suit the needs of the hour, but it was not destined to be put into practice in South Wales. For it was Ostorius who died 'worn out with the burden of his cares'. Tacitus does not fail to record the joy of the Silures, who took pride in the thought that they had 'destroyed a formidable adversary, if not in battle, then at least in the course of war'. They were entitled to congratulate themselves. We, too, should pause at this moment of success for the Silures, to reflect that we do not know the name of a single one of their leaders. This is a pity, because as 'patriot chiefs' they take rank beside Caratacus and Boudicca; indeed, the successes they won against the Roman army in the field are unparalleled by any British people before the wars of the second century A.D. in Caledonia and Brigantia. As a result of their efforts against Ostorius, their people retained their identity, to become, in the end, a *civitas* of the Roman province. Their descendants still live in the land, and, though their name is now used only in a specialist context,[7] those who go to play Rugby football in South Wales will testify that their *pervicacia* is well maintained.

The death of Ostorius at this juncture meant a grave emergency for the Roman government, reflected in Tacitus' words 'when the death of the Governor became known, Claudius sent in his place [*suffecit*] Aulus Didius [Gallus] lest the province should be without a ruler'. The statement is less straightforward than might appear, for it is obvious that Britain must have a governor: to labour the point is to suggest that the emergency explains, but does not justify, the choice of Didius Gallus. We are primed for the disparaging comments which, on no fewer than four occasions, Tacitus goes out of his way to make on Didius' conduct of British affairs. And what is the point of *suffecit*, since that verb is normally used of appointments made to an office whose holder's term has not expired? It implies, perhaps, that Ostorius was due to retire in 53, and that one of the consuls of 52 was already marked to succeed him. For some reason this man could not be released on Ostorius' death, but Didius Gallus was in Rome and available, though at his age he would not normally have expected another provincial command. History and epigraphy tell us enough of the career of the third Governor of Britain to discount some of Tacitus' settled bias against him. *Consul suffectus* in A.D. 36, he probably accompanied Claudius to Britain in A.D. 43, and may have held a special cavalry command. His next appointment took him from the north-west to the north-east of the Roman Empire, for he became Governor of Moesia. As such he had to deal with troubles in two client-kingdoms, Thrace and Bosporus. In both a mixture of war and diplomacy produced a solution favourable to Rome, and Didius was awarded *ornamenta triumphalia*. Later he held a senatorial province, but it was this Moesian command which made him a good appointment for Britain at this time. Tacitus, it should be admitted, is not his only critic, for there is a story in Quintilian[8] of a rebuke administered to him as being more concerned for his own interests, rather than those of the State, in canvassing with excessive zeal for a provincial command, which could well have been that of Britain at the death of Ostorius.

Certainly Didius, by the year A.D. 52, was 'full of honours', but if this made him indolent it did not appear to the outset. Hastening to Britain, he found that the situation, bad enough at the death of Ostorius, had deteriorated further, and was now out of military control. The Silures had defeated a legion, 'under the command of Manlius Valens'—and presumably the XXth—and now they were ravaging far and wide in the province. In other words, the defences along the lower Severn had collapsed, and the Roman units were pinned within their forts, as they were to be later in the early phase of Boudicca's rebellion. (The name of the commander is given with a purpose. The defeat by the Silures would seem to have damaged Manlius Valens' whole career. In A.D. 69 he is still no more than a legionary commander—the oldest known. He was to go on to a second and more notable record, for in A.D. 96 he became the oldest man ever to hold the consulship—at the age of 89!)[9] Tacitus is at pains to play down the situation—'the report [of the defeat]', he says, 'was exaggerated, first by the enemy to alarm the incoming governor, and secondly by Didius . . . so as to gain greater credit if he settled the situation, and to have a better excuse, if it persisted. To this tangle of motives we may fairly add another—the desire of Tacitus to discredit Didius. Perhaps Manlius Valens was his source? Tacitus was consul in A.D. 97; he may well have heard the old gentleman, still embittered over memories of the débâcle in Britain more than forty years ago. Even so, Tacitus cannot deny that Didius achieved a rapid solution. 'On his arrival the Silures were expelled from the province.' Since we do not hear of them again for four or five years, it would seem that they took a hard knock in the process. And if Didius made no gains in Silurian territory as a result, he may only have been obeying instructions. In any case, two unforeseen and serious events ruled out any adventures in Wales during his term of office.

The first of these was the murder of Claudius at the instigation of his wife Agrippina in A.D. 54. It brought to power a new administration under a young and untried *princeps*: some of Claudius' policies, and many of his advisers, were discarded. Prominent among the latter was Narcissus, who had been so closely identified with the invasion of Britain. The current line in imperial propaganda was to portray Nero as the new Augustus; a return to the Augustan frontiers would have been in keeping with this policy. Here, in the early years of Nero, is the best context for Suetonius' statement that that emperor once contemplated a withdrawal from Britain. Didius Gallus, obviously, could make no forward move until this cardinal decision had been made. The remainder of his office would presumably have been quiet, but for events beyond his control in Brigantia. Queen Cartimandua had been well paid for her loyalty to Rome when she handed over Caratacus. She gained wealth, as one might expect, but Tacitus is at pains to emphasise that she also gained power (*auxerat potentiam*).[10] This suggests an expansion of the southern kingdom, over which Cartimandua ruled directly, at the expense of the northern Brigantian realm of her husband Venutius. It is unlikely, however, that she had gained in the respect of her subjects, and Venutius' resentment, combined with that of the anti-Roman faction in the state, led to an outburst of civil war that called for Roman intervention. It is unfortunate that Tacitus did not choose to work up the Cartimandua story, but he discloses enough to show that it had all the makings of a great Celtic heroic tale. Cartimandua was wealthy and cruel, lustful and treacherous—a Clytemnestra of a woman. She had captured Caratacus by guile, now she employed the same deceitful arts to get Venutius' brother and kinsmen in her power. Venutius himself was a formidable figure—the greatest military chieftain in Britain, now that Caratacus was gone.[11] He could plan boldly and muster a great force—witness the enormous earthworks at Stanwick (137 acres, later enlarged to over 600), where his followers gathered in the last phases of the struggle for Brigantian independence.[12] Cartimandua's insolence, and this latest aggression, were more than he could stomach, even though it brought him into collision with Rome. And now his reaction was swift and characteristic: 'a powerful band of young warriors'—the royal war-band, in fact—'invaded her kingdom',[13] the object being, no doubt, to rescue Venutius' kinsmen, and perhaps to capture the Queen. The heroic world of northern Britain was much the same five centuries later, when the *teulu* or war-band of Mynyddawg Mwynfawr, lord of Edinburgh, 'went to Catraeth' to make their famous raid on the English settled at Catterick in the ruins of the old Roman town. Thanks to the poet Aneirin, we know much of their deeds—'three hundred warriors went to Catraeth, and of all that host but one man came back alive'.[14] But—'they killed seven times their number of English'.

How many were in the war-band of Venutius we cannot say, but its movements were known to the Roman command, and help was ready for Cartimandua when the situation looked like getting out of hand. Didius Gallus by now was too old and infirm for campaigning in the Pennines, which dates the Brigantian civil war late in his governorship, in 55, or more probably 56. He was forced to act through subordinates, which meant that operations were in charge of the legionary commander Caesius Nasica. Again, the name has significance, for Caesius Nasica was probably the brother of Petilius Cerealis, who later (c. A.D. 60) held the same command at Lincoln, and as governor of Britain carried out the conquest of the Brigantes

176

(71–4).[15] His command was, almost certainly, the IXth Legion at Lincoln, and the campaigns that follow are the first in which we can identify that legion in action. It was thought at first that auxiliary units would be sufficient, but those sent to support the Queen had to fight a fierce action, which only in its last phases went in their favour. Their victory—if such it was—did not end the campaign, and the legion itself had to take the field and fight another hard battle. Since the war-band can hardly have been numerous enough to face a Roman legion, it looks as though Venutius had followed up with his main army. This is all that Tacitus has to tell about the military side of the war against the Brigantes, and of the diplomatic sequel he says nothing. Yet once more, as with the Silures, a satisfactory solution was apparently reached. Cartimandua retained her kindgom, and Venutius his: for the war had begun as a Brigantian affair, not as a move against Rome. Even their divorce was some years in the future, and if Venutius by now cherished a vendetta against Cartimandua and a hatred for Rome,[16] he had to wait to express them until an hour of graver weakness than Didius Gallus can have foreseen. The crucial test, surely, of the settlement lay in the fact that when the rebellion of Boudicca broke out only a few years later, Cartimandua was able to prevent her people from going over to the rebel cause. The Brigantian problem was the last that Didius Gallus handled in a long and honourable career: there is no indication that he bungled it.

If it was hard to place the events in South Wales on the map, it is harder still here in the north. If we could be sure that Cartimandua's capital was at the northern Camulodunum (Almondbury), it is somewhere near the modern Huddersfield that we should look for the scene of the fierce action between the Brigantian war-band and the Roman auxiliaries. As for the legionary battle, the Brigantian fortress at Stanwick and the Roman legionary base at York were both later to attest to the importance of the natural line of penetration along the east flank of the Pennines. Somewhere between York and Catterick would be the likely scene of the battle where Caesius Nasica met and turned back the army of the northern king.

One further feature of Didius Gallus' work may be deduced from Tacitus. In the *Agricola* he makes the familiar charge that Didius

Gallus did no more than maintain the ground won by his predecessors, adding the contemptuous phrase that 'by founding a small number of forts in the remoter parts of the province he sought to win a reputation for having enlarged the duty entrusted to him'.[17] Now it seems unlikely that Didius Gallus can have retained, let alone extended, the system of forts in Silurian territory built up by Scapula. But the situation in Brigantia at the end of Didius' term of office would seem to demand just such an extension as Tacitus has described. It has been observed that there are signs of an early fort at Little Chester, and certainly that place was a nodal point in the later system of roads and forts in the Peak. But the object of this system was to control the native peoples of the Peak, and to protect the rear of the strategic road connecting the legionary bases at York and Chester. To protect the kingdom of Cartimandua against an attack from the north it would be imperative to have a firm grip on the Ouse Valley. Here again one thinks of York, which has yielded some pre-Flavian objects, which may indicate military occupation earlier than the legionary fortress of A.D. 71.[18] Didius Gallus may well have been the first Roman governor to realise the importance of this great strategic centre of the north. The legionary base, of course, remained at Lincoln in his time and for more than a decade afterwards. This being so, one looks with interest at the road leading north-west from Lincoln to the Pennine fringe, and marked by later forts at Bawtry, Doncaster, and Castleford. A little to the south-west of this line the fort at Templeborough has been dated to about A.D. 60.[19]

While these events were taking place in Brigantia, the government of Nero had reached its decision about Britain. There was to be no withdrawal. Its implications were that the Claudian policy of limited conquest in the lowland zone of England would have to be discarded. Confronted with the geographical and political realities of Britain, it had shown itself to be inadequate. The security of the province would demand at least the conquest of Wales; flaws had shown themselves in the policy of supporting a client-kingdom in Brigantia, but for the time it would be allowed to stand. A new governor would clearly be needed, and with the hour came the man. Quintus Veranius, in his mid-forties, with a fine military record in Lycia and

Pamphylia, viewed his task with enthusiasm and confidence—and was destined to die within a year.[20]

We have already reviewed the many checks and delays encountered by the Neronian forward policy, which was not to be implemented until the succession of able governors under Vespasian. Thus the problems of Wales and Brigantia remained open for almost two decades after Claudius. With the eighties came Agricola's audacious but unsuccessful project for the conquest of Caledonia. Once this was abandoned, a northern *limes* had to be established—hence the vast and expensive schemes of Hadrian and Antoninus Pius. Behind these barriers the Roman province prospered until the troubles of the later fourth century. Even so, this northern British *limes* was always one of the most warlike frontiers of the Empire, and was breached several times. Add to all this the known troubles in Brigantia in the second century, and the archaeological evidence, substantial and still growing, that Wales was restless at that time.[21] The example of Caratacus was not in vain. At all times in Britain, within and without the Roman province, there were to be men who preferred *libertas* to *pax*.

APPENDIX I

The Narrative of
Dio Cassius, LX, 19–22

§ 19. ... At about this time Aulus Plautius, a distinguished Senator,
commanded an expedition to Britain. For a certain Bericus, expelled
from the island by internal strife, had persuaded Claudius to dispatch
a force there. That is how Aulus Plautius came to command an
invading army, but it was with great difficulty that he led his army
out of Gaul. The soldiers grumbled at having to campaign outside
the inhabited world (as they put it), and they refused to listen to him
until Narcissus, who had been sent by Claudius, mounted the commander's platform and began to address them. At this point they
were still more annoyed with Aulus Plautius and disinclined to let
Narcissus utter a word: but all of a sudden they shouted out aloud
the well-known cry '*Io Saturnalia!*' (this because at the festival of
Saturn the slaves dress up in their masters' clothes to keep holiday).
After this they readily obeyed Plautius' orders. But the delay had
postponed their sailing-date until late in the season: they sailed in
three divisions to avoid the delays in landing which might be
occasioned by the ferrying over of a single force. Their crossing was
at first discouraging because contrary winds drove them back, but
eventually they were cheered by a brilliant flash of light which
appeared in the east and shot across the sky to the west—the direction of their course. They landed on the island without opposition,
for the reports which reached the Britons had led them to suppose
that the Romans would not come—consequently they had not
mustered. Even at this stage they declined to meet them in the field,
but took refuge in the swamps and forests, hoping in this way so to
wear them down that they would sail away with nothing achieved—
precisely as had happened in the case of Julius Caesar.

§ 20. Aulus Plautius therefore had much trouble in making contact
with them. When he did so, he defeated first Caratacus and then
Togodumnus, the sons of Cunobelinus, who was dead. (At this
period the Britons were not free and independent, but ruled by the

kings of other tribes.) When these kings had fled he won over by agreement a portion of the Bodunni [*sic*], a people dependent on the Catuvellauni; thereupon he left a garrison there and continued his advance. Then he came to a river. The Britons supposed that the Romans would not be able to cross it without a bridge, and so had encamped carelessly on the opposite bank. He therefore sent across Gallic troops who were trained to swim with full equipment across the swiftest of rivers. Surprise was achieved against the enemy by this attack: but they did not shoot at the men themselves: instead, wounding the horses that drew their chariots, they made it impossible even for the charioteers to get away in the subsequent confusion. At this point Plautius sent over Vespasian (the future Emperor), and his brother Sabinus, who was serving under his command. This force also succeeded in crossing the river, and killing many of the barbarians, who were not expecting them. The rest of the British forces did not retreat, however, but remained to fight on the following day. There was an indecisive struggle, but at last Gnaeus Hosidius Geta (after being almost taken prisoner) managed to defeat them. For this achievement he was later awarded *ornamenta triumphalia*, though he had never been consul. Then the Britons fell back from this position on to the River Thames, at a point where it enters the sea and forms a large pool at high tide. Knowing the firm ground and the fords with much precision, they crossed the river without difficulty, but the Roman forces were not so successful. However, the Celts (i.e. auxiliaries) swam across again, and some others got over by a bridge a little way upstream, after which they assailed the barbarians from several sides at once and cut down many of them. But they were incautious in their pursuit of the rest, got themselves trapped in impassable marshes, and lost many of their men.

§ 21. Shortly after this Togodumnus died. Far from giving in, the Britons gathered all the more stubbornly to avenge him. Plautius became alarmed and refused to advance further. Resolved to hold on to ground he had already won, he sent for Claudius. Indeed, his instructions had been to do precisely this if anything untoward should happen: substantial preparation had been made for reinforcements, including troops and elephants.

When the message reached him, Claudius entrusted affairs at Rome (including the command of the troops, i.e. that part of the Praetorian Guard left in Rome, its commander Rufrius Pollio accompanying Claudius to Britain) to his colleague in the consulship, Lucius Vitellius, who like himself had served a full six months in office, and set out for the campaign. Sailing down the river to Ostia, he voyaged thence to Massilia; then he went across Gaul by road and river to the Ocean. Crossing the Channel, he joined the troops who had been awaiting him on the Thames. Taking them with him he crossed the river, engaged the barbarians who had gathered to dispute his advance, gained the victory, and captured Camulodunon, the royal seat of Cunobelinus. Later he won over numerous tribes—some by battle, some by negotiation—and was hailed 'imperator' several times—contrary to custom, for the rule was that none should receive this acclamation more than once in any one campaign. Disarming these tribes, he handed them over to Aulus Plautius, who received instructions to subdue the remainder of the country. He then left for Rome, having sent ahead news of his victory by Magnus and Silanus, his sons-in-law.

§ 22. On hearing of his achievement the Senate voted him the title of Britannicus, and gave permission for him to celebrate a Triumph. They further approved an annual festival of commemoration and the erection of two triumphal arches, one in Rome, and one in Gaul at the place where he had crossed over to Britain. The title of Britannicus was also conferred on his son: indeed, it became his usual name. Messalina received the same seat of honour at the theatre that had been granted to Livia, and also the privilege of using a town carriage.*

* The *carpentum* was a covered carriage. Only the Empress and the Vestal Virgins had the privilege of using it, as an exception from the traffic regulations forbidding the use of wheeled vehicles in the city during daylight hours.

APPENDIX II

The Chichester Inscription

The Chichester inscription, on a Purbeck marble slab 5 ft 3 in by 2 ft 7 in, was found in four pieces which have since suffered from weathering and damage, and reads as follows*:

N]EPTVNO ET MINERVAE
  TEMPLVM
PR]O SALVTE DO[MVS] DIVINAE
EX] AVCTORITAT[E T]I CLAVD
CO]GIDVBNI R L[EGAT] AVG IN BRIT
COLLE]GIVM FABROR [ET QV]I IN EO
SVNT] D S D DONANTE AREAM
CLEM]ENTE PVDENTINI FIL

Expanded form:

NEPTVNO ET MINERVAE
  TEMPLVM
PRO SALVTE DOMVS DIVINAE
EX AVCTORITATE TI(BERII) CLAVDII
COGIDVBNI R(EGIS) LEGAT(I) AVG(VSTI) IN
                          BRIT(ANNIA)
COLLEGIVM FABRORVM ET QVI IN EO
SVNT DE SVO DEDERVNT DONANTE AREAM
CLEMENTE PVDENTINI FILIO

Meaning:

A temple to Neptune, Minerva and for the well-being of the Divine House [of the Emperor] by the authority of King Tiberius Claudius Cogidubnus Imperial Legate in Britain [erected by] the gild of artisans and its members at their own cost. Clemens son of Pudentinus donated the site.

* This reading was suggested by R. G. Collingwood (Tacitus, *de vita Agricolae*, ed. Furneaux, revised by J. G. C. Anderson, 1922, 79; see also *V.C.H., Sussex*, iii, 1935, 13).

APPENDIX III
The Dedicatory Inscription
(*C.I.L.*VI 920) on the Arch of Claudius

The surviving portion of the inscription is illustrated in figure *43*; the restoration below.* The translation is as follows:

> To the Emperor Tiberius Claudius, son of Drusus, Caesar Augustus Germanicus, Pontifex Maximus, Tribunician power for the eleventh time, Consul for the fifth time, saluted as Imperator twenty-two (?) times, Censor, Father of his Country. [Set up by] the Senate and People of Rome because he received the formal submission of eleven Kings of the Britons, overcome without any loss, and because he was the first to bring barbarian peoples across the Ocean under the sway of the Roman people.

Three points concern us here: the eleven British kings, the phrase *sine ulla iactura*, and the reference to the Ocean. The figure of XI is certain, the problem is to identify the British kings concerned. Caratacus can hardly be included. He had been defeated before the dedication of the Arch (A.D. 52), but the phrase *sine ulla iactura* loses meaning if it has to cover the man who, in Tacitus' words, 'had defied Roman power for so many years'. Nor can we safely suppose the words that *devictos . . . in deditionem acceperit* apply only to those

---

* See further, F. Castagnoli, *Bolletino della Commissione Archeologica del Governatoro di Roma*, LXX (1942), pp. 57–82: D. R. Dudley, *University of Birmingham Historical Journal* VII, no. 1 (1959), 11 ff.

defeated in battle: they are used of formal acts of submission, whether voluntary or after defeat in war. The eleven kings named therefore appear to be those who, whether after defeat or negotiation, made their surrender in person to Claudius at Colchester. Presumably they include Cogidubnus, Prasutagus (or another king of the Iceni), and the ruler of the Brigantes (Cartimandua?). Kings of the Coritani and Dobunni may also be suggested: perhaps too there were rulers to surrender on behalf of the Catuvellauni and Trinovantes; the Kentish tribes, the Cornovii, and the Parisii are also possibles. All we can really say is that the XI of the inscription is the kind of figure to be expected from what we know of the campaigns. The word *iactura* appears to be deliberately chosen as a word of wide meaning, and the whole phrase, taken closely with the surrender of the eleven kings, is to imply that Claudius' conduct of operations in Britain met with no reverse or setback. There is little doubt that it is meant to point the contrast with the fiasco of Gaius, exactly as the arch of Claudius at Gesoriacum (Boulogne) commemorates an authentic victory in the traditional Roman manner, in contrast to the 'lighthouse' (or trophy?) of Gaius. The claim that Claudius was the 'first to bring barbarian peoples across the Ocean under the sway of the Roman people' is a simple statement of fact, if we take it to refer to the establishment of a Roman province in Britain. A passage from Claudius' 'Speech to the Gauls'† makes it clear that the Emperor saw this as the culminating achievement of Roman history 'I am afraid that... if I mention the wars we have successfully undertaken, I shall seem too immoderate, in having sought to make a display of the glory we have won by extending the Empire across the Ocean.' Scramuzza‡ has shown in detail how these British conquests of Claudius round off the work of his kinsmen in the lands surrounding the North Sea.

It should be added that the Arch at Cyzicus: *C.I.L.*, III, S. 7061 (=Dessau *I.L.S.*, 217), set up for reasons of local politics, selects only the surrender of the eleven kings, and says nothing about the 'Conquest of the Ocean'.

† M. P. Charlesworth, *Documents to illustrate the reigns of Claudius and Nero* (Cambridge, 1939), 9.
‡ V. Scramuzza, *The Emperor Claudius*, 205, 308.

43 The inscription from Chichester, giving the name and titles of Cogidubnus

(See Appendix II, p. 184)

44 The extant part of the inscription from the Arch of Claudius

(See Appendix III, p. 185)

45–7   *Three military tombstones from Wroxeter (See Appendix IV, p. 189)*

APPENDIX IV

Military Tombstones

Two military tombstones from Colchester (figs. 2 and 4)

1 Found in 1884 in Beverley Road along the presumed course of the Roman road from London. It reads:

M(ARCVS) FĀVON(IVS) M(ARCI) F(ILIVS) POL(LIA) FACI

LIS · > LEG(IONIS) XX · VERECVN͡D
VS ET NOVICIVS LIB(ERTI) POS
ERVNT · H(IC) S(ITVS) E(ST)

Marcus Favonius Facilis, son of Marcus, of the Pollian tribe, centurion of the XXth Legion, erected by Verecundus and Novicius his freedmen. He is buried here. (*C.I.L.*, vii, 90.)

2 Found in 1928 in Beverley Road near the site of the above where early graves have been noted (*Roman Colchester*, 1959, p. 251). The inscription below the relief tells us that it is the tombstone of Longinus, son of Sdapezematygus, a *duplicarius* of the first Thracian *ala*, born in Sardica (now Sofia in Bulgaria), died in his fortieth year and fifteenth year of service. He wears a jerkin of large scales and his sturdy horse is finely caparisoned. The stone suffered damage, presumably in the revolt of Boudicca in A.D. 60 when the face was smashed, the lance knocked off and the stone overthrown. (*J.R.S.*, 18 (1928), p. 212; *Trans. Essex Arch. Soc.*, 19.2, pp. 1–6.)

3 *A legionary tombstone from Mainz (fig. 3)*

It reads:

P(UBLIUS) FLAVOLEIUS . P(UBLII) . F(ILIUS) .
   POL(LIA) .
MUTINA . CORDUS . MIL(ES) .
LEG(IONIS) . XIIII . GEM(INAE) . H(IC) . S(ITUS) .
   E(ST) .

ANN(ORUM) . XLIII . STIP(ENDIORUM) . XXIII .
C(AIUS) .
VIBENNIUS . L(UCII) . F(ILIUS) . EX.T(ESTAMENTO) .
FEC(IT)

Publius Flavoleius Cordus, son of Publius, of the Pollian tribe, born at Mutina (Modena in Northern Italy), soldier of the XIVth Legion *Gemina*. Here is the place. 43 years old, 23 years service. Erected by Caius Vibennius, son of Lucius, according to the provisions of the will. (*C.I.L.,* xiii, 7255.)

Cordus is shown in his undress uniform holding his *pilum,* which has suffered damage, and a scroll, presumably denoting his citizenship. Details of the dagger (*pugio*) and military belt are very clear. The shield slung on his back is the mason's representation of the normal semi-cylindrical type.

A military tombstone from Cirencester (fig. 5)

4 Found in 1836 in Watermoor to the south of the Roman town. (*Arch.* 27, 215; 69, 186; *C.I.L.,* vii, 68.) The inscription tells us that the tombstone is that of Sextus Valerius Genialis, a trooper of a Thracian *ala,* born in Frisia (now north-eastern Holland). Although Genialis is described as a trooper (*eques*) he carries in addition to the oval shield a device which appears to be some kind of standard but not the usual cavalry flag (*vexillum*). He wears an elaborate helmet but damage to the stone prevents it being positively identified as one of those used on parade, with a face-visor similar to that from Ribchester in the British Museum (*Art in Roman Britain,* 1962, No. 108). On his jerkin is an emblem which may have represented a Medusa head, thought to give protection.

Three military tombstones from Wroxeter (figs. 44–6)

5 Found in 1752 in a field nearly a mile from Wroxeter village, about 200 yards from the foundation of the Roman town wall on the north-east towards Watling Street. It reads:

M(ARCVS) PETRONIVS L(VCII) F(ILIVS) MEN(ENIA
TRIBV) VIC(ETIA). ANN(ORVM) XXXVIII MIL(ES)

LEG(IONIS) XIIII GEM(INAE) MILITAVIT ANN(OS)
XVIII
SIGN(IFER) FVIT H(IC) S(ITVS) E(ST).

Marcus Petronius, son of Lucius, of the Menenian tribe (all
Roman citizens belonged to a tribe for voting purposes), born
at Vicetia (Vicenza, in Northern Italy), 38 years old, a soldier
of the XIVth Legion *Gemina*. He served 18 years, he was a
standard bearer. He is buried here. (*C.I.L.,* vii, 155.)

6   Found with No. 5 and reads:

C(AIVS) MANNIVS C(AI) F(ILIVS) POL(LIA) SECVNDVS
POLLEN(TIA) MIL(ES) LEG(IONIS) XX AN(N)ORV(M)
LII
STIP(ENDIORVM) XXXI BEN(EFICIARIVS) LEG(ATI)
PR(OVINCIAE) H(IC) S(ITVS) E(ST)

Caius Mannius Secundus, son of Caius, of the Pollian tribe,
born at Pollentia (near Turin in Northern Italy), a soldier of
the XXth Legion, 52 years old, 31 years service, an orderly of
the governor of the province. He is buried here. (*C.I.L.,* vii,
156.)

7   Found about the same time as Nos 5 and 6 and reads:

TIB(ERIVS) CLAUD(IVS) TIR[.]NTIVS EQ(VES)
COH(ORTIS)
... THRACVM ANNORVM LVII STIPENDIORVM ...
H(IC) S(ITVS) E(ST)
Tiberius Claudius Tir[.]ntius, a trooper of the (?) Cohort of
Thracians, 57 years old, (?) years service. He is buried here.
(*C.I.L.,* vii, 158.)

APPENDIX V
Chichester: Items of Military Equipment in the Sadler Collection

1. Belt plate with hook decorated with winding scrolls with small leaves. This is a typical piece of decoration from a legionary belt, cf. similar examples from Hod Hill (*B.M. Guide* (1922) Fig. 105a and f); Richborough (*IV*, Pl. xxxiii, No. 72); Hofheim (Taf. xii, Nos. 1–7); Mainz (*M.Z.*, vii (1912) Abb. 4, Nos. 23 and 24); *Verulamium* (*Arch.*, 90 (1944) Fig. 4, No. 11); Weymouth (B.M. Durden Coll., Acc. No. 9–1, 1705) etc.

2. Belt or apron plate with corroded surface which has removed the original niello decoration, cf. Hofheim (Taf. xii, No. 21; xv, No. 94), there are other examples in the Guildhall Museum, London (Acc. No. 4444) and Wroxeter (in Site Museum).

3. Buckle with traces of silvering, a typical military buckle, cf. Novaesium (Taf. xxx, No. 73); Hofheim (Taf. xi, No. 31); Wiesbaden (*O-R.L.*, No. 31, Taf. x, No. 33); Mainz (*M.Z.*, vii (1912) Abb. 3, No. 15); *Camulodunum* (Pl. cii, Nos. 20 and 21) Ham Hill (*Proc. Somerset Arch. Soc.*, lxix (1923) Pl. xi, No. 6).

4. Silvered toggle end of belt or baldric. A similar form of fastener comes from the Walbrook, London (*Small finds from Walbrook 1954–55*, Pl. iii, No. 7) cf. also Zugmantel (*O-R.L.*, No. 8, Taf. xxi, No. 45).

5. Part of cuirass hook flattened out, the function of these hooks is the fastening of the *lorica segmenta*, as demonstrated by van Groller (*R.L.O.*, ii, Text fig. 24).

6. Two small domed studs with niello for attachment to belt mounts, there are precise parallels from Hofheim (Taf. xii, Nos. 40–44).

7. A small conical stud with traces of a lion mask (?) from a mount or pendant. Similar to examples from *Novaesium* (Taf. xxx, Nos. 25 and 26) and Kastell Pfünz (*O-R.L.*, No. 73, Taf. xiii, No. 43).

8. A small fragment of thin bronze with central hole and circular moulded decoration. This may be a seal-box lid or a mount for bronze or leather.

9. Small twisted piece of a bronze strap fastener with copper rivets similar to those used on the *lorica segmentata*, cf. part of a strap in the Guildhall Museum, London (Acc. No. 14,283).

10. Lancing Down pendant from the Medhurst Coll., *Gents Mag.*, July 1886 (Ashmolean Museum Acc. No. 1927.6436), illustrated in E. T. Leeds, *Celtic Ornament*, 1933, fig. 30b.

APPENDIX VI

The Seven Sisters Hoard

The Seven Sisters hoard (*41*) was found at Nant-y cefn in the Vale of Neath, Glamorgan, in 1875 but the collection did not finally reach the National Museum of Wales until 1904, after which it was published by Romilly Allen (*Arch. Camb.*, 1905, pp. 127-146). Among the twenty objects recovered are six tankard handles and six pieces of horse gear decorated with enamel. Ten of the other items are undoubtedly of Roman military origin typical of the middle of the first century but the Celtic character of the remainder has led to the belief that much of the hoard is of native origin. (Hence it was included by W. F. Grimes in his *Guide to the Collections illustrating the Prehistory of Wales*, 1939, Fig. 40 on p. 195.) The poor decoration of the enamelled pieces has, however, lost much of its Celtic flavour. They are comparable to similar objects found in Roman contexts (e.g. Waddon Hill in Dorset, Carlisle and Inchtuthil, all as yet unpublished). It is the kind of work one might expect from British craftsmen obliged to mass-produce their wares for the Roman Army. It is suggested that the whole of this hoard may have been part of the spoils from a sacked fort or beaten cavalry unit. An exception might be made for the tankard handles but even these are not unknown in Roman forts (*Antiquities from the Hod Hill in the Druden Collection*, 1962, Fig. 14, nos. 1, 5 and 6 and plate X; Waddon Hill, Dorset, *Proc. Prehist. Soc.*, 17 (1952), Pl. X, No. 3, and *Proc. Dorset Nat. Hist. and Arch. Soc.*, 82 (1961), Fig. 10; and a later example from Newstead, *A Roman Frontier Post and its People*, 1911, Pl. LIV, No. 7). A wooden tankard, adorned with these handles, was a useful and decorative item a Roman soldier would have purchased from a British craftsman or taken as loot.

Notes and References

CHAPTER 1

1. If indeed the Hosidius Geta who served in Mauretania is the same person: he may have been a brother of the Geta who came to Britain

2. Caesar, *De Bello Gallico* (referred to below as *D.B.G.*), iv, 22; v, 8

3. Dessau, *Inscriptiones Latinae Selectae* (referred to below as *I.L.S.*), 970; *Année Épigraphique* (1947), No. 76 and 1949, No. 11

4. *Classical Quarterly*, 13 (1963), 269

5. Dio Cassius, lx, 20. Tacitus frequently mentions these units, whose skill and fighting qualities seem to have impressed him

6. '*Insularum quas Romana notitia complectitur maxima*', Tacitus, *Agricola*, 10

7. *Annals*, ii, 33 ff

8. It is highly probable that some of them will have taken part in the abortive expedition of Gaius. J. P. V. Balsdon, 'Notes concerning the Principate of Gaius', *J.R.S.*, 24 (1934), 13–24

9. Dio Cassius, lx, 19

10. J. P. V. Balsdon, *J.R.S.*, 24 (1934), 17

11. G. L. Cheesman, *The Auxilia of the Roman Army* (1914)

12. There is a tiny fragment from one such inscription of the early second century from the turf section of Hadrian's Wall, recognised and brilliantly interpreted by R. G. Collingwood, *Cumberland and Westmorland Trans.*, 35 (1935), 220

13. C. G. Starr, *Roman Imperial Navy 31 B.C.—A.D. 324* (2nd Ed., 1960)

14. *Annals*, ii, 6

15. Caesar, *D.B.G.*, iv, 32

16. Sir Cyril Fox, *A Find of the Early Iron Age from Llyn Cerrig Bach, Anglesey* (National Museum of Wales 1946)

17. *Ant. J.,* 27 (1947), 117–19
18. Caesar's British expeditions are described in *De Bello Gallico* iv, 20–36, and v, 8–23. The best discussion of the problems raised is still that of Rice Holmes in *Ancient Britain and the Invasions of Julius Caesar* (Oxford, 1907), though many of his views would not be accepted by modern scholars
19. See on this A. N. Sherwin-White, *Greece and Rome*, Vol. IV, No. 1 (Julius Caesar Bimillenary Number) 36–45
20. For possible political reasons see C. E. Stevens, *Antiquity* XXI (1947), 3–9
21. *Verulamium, A Belgic and Two Roman Cities* (1936), 16–22

CHAPTER 2

1. The Celtic name is Camulodunon
2. lv, 5, 1–2
3. C. F. C. Hawkes and M. R. Hull, *Camulodunum* (1947)
4. Suetonius, *Caligula*, 44, 2
5. See D. F. Allen, 'The Belgic dynasties of Britain and their Coins', *Archaeologia*, 90 (1944), 1–46
6. R. P. Mack, *The Coinage of Ancient Britain* (1953), no. 265 and p. 58. They are inscribed CARA and are identical in type to the silver issue of Epaticcus
7. Dio Cassius, lx, 19
8. Tacitus, *Agricola*, 24
9. Suetonius, *Claudius*, 17
10. *Cambridge Antiquarian Soc. Proc.*, 50 (1956), 1–27; evidence from the excavation of Wandlebury
11. See I. A. Richmond, 'The Cornovii', in *Culture and Environment* (1963), 251 ff
12. *Agricola*, 11
13. Strabo, iv, 5, 1–3. It should be noted that the *Res Gestae* of Augustus (vi, 32) records the names of two British princes,

Dumnobellaunus and Tincommius, among suppliants seeking his friendship

14. By C. E. Stevens in *Aspects of Archaeology in Britain and Beyond* (1951), 340
15. Dio Cassius, lx, 23, 6
16. *Annals*, xii, 37
17. Caesar, *D.B.G.*, i, 29
18. Diodorus Siculus, v, 25
19. *Annals*, xii, 34; *Agricola*, 15
20. Strabo, iv, 2, 3
21. Probably the best modern discussion is by A. Momigliano, *Claudius* (reprinted 1961)

CHAPTER 3

1. Dio Cassius, lx, 19–22, gives a narrative of the campaign
2. *C.I.L.*, vi, 920: 31203; *C.I.L.*, iii, 7061. See further pp. 185f
3. Suetonius, *Claudius*, 17; *Vespasian*, 4
4. Caesar, *D.B.G.*, iv, 25
5. Tacitus, *Agricola*, 14
6. We owe much in what follows to our discussion with Professor Birley
7. Professor Birley has pointed out (*Sussex Arch. Coll.*, 94 (1956), 102) that the first of a new series of judicial officers, C. Salvius Liberalis, was appointed to Britain *c.* A.D. 78. This may have been as a result of the death of the king and the consequent absorption of the kingdom into the province in an equitable and peaceful manner, avoiding the holocaust at the death of Prasutagus, the King of the Iceni
8. By Professor C. F. C. Hawkes, at the suggestion of Mr C. E. Stevens, in *Bagendon, A Belgic Oppidum* (1961), 65
9. *Breviarium Historiae Romanae*, vii, 13
10. He had at the death of Gaius proposed in the Senate a return to the Republic

11. Directed by J. P. Bushe-Fox for the Society of Antiquaries, *Fourth Report on the Excavations of the Roman Fort at Richborough, Kent* (1949). A fifth Report is forthcoming

12. There is, however, a difficulty in the discovery of a gateway at the entrance. This consists of the remains of four post-pits and suggestions of two others arranged in the pattern one normally associates with a military gate. If these represent the remains of a substantial wooden structure protecting the entrance to the camp, it would appear to be of more permanent and of longer duration than our previous argument would allow. The excavator was uncertain about these finds and is at pains to point out that 'no definite proof could be obtained that these were of the same date as the Claudian defences, but they do not appear to belong to the later buildings and their central position in the entrance passage points to some connection with it'. There is yet another piece of evidence recorded by the excavator which may throw doubt on the connection of the 'gate' with the camp. The post-pits were filled with decayed turf and he states that the wooden uprights 'had been packed round with rammed sand and turf'. This could not have happened if the gate-posts had been erected as part of the original defences, since the post-pits would have been packed with the clean material dug out of the holes, and this is usually well-rammed and sterile. The presence of turf seems to indicate that the erection of this timber structure took place after the turf rampart of the camp went out of use and could be used for filling in these holes. The timbers could have belonged to the buildings subsequently erected and there is nothing in the general plan (Pl. xcvi) which would militate against this idea. There is yet another possibility that the turves occurred only in the trenches cut into the post-pits when the wooden uprights were removed, and this might also account for the irregular shape of the post-pits which if undisturbed are normally of neat rectangular plan. This suggestion would explain the shape of the one post-pit illustrated by a photograph (Pl. iv a)

13. Although the part plans of only four of these granaries have been published, more were identified and will appear in the fifth Report, together it is hoped with a general plan showing the relationships with all these timber buildings

14. *Roman Britain and the English Settlements* (2nd ed., 1937), 81

15. Professor C. F. C. Hawkes in *Bagendon, A Belgic Oppidum* (1961), 60

16. It was not unusual for high ranking officers and officials to be accompanied by relations and friends who assisted in an unofficial capacity. Sabinus was senior to Vespasian and more advanced in his career at this stage

17. A. R. Burn, 'The Battle of the Medway, A.D. 43', *History*, 39 (1953), 105–15

18. Professor Birley informs us that Geta may have had six years seniority over Vespasian

19. *Numismatic Chronicle*, 6th Ser., 19 (1959), 17

20. Sir Cyril Fox, *A Find of the Early Iron Age from Llyn Cerrig Bach, Anglesey* (1946)

21. R. C. Collingwood, *Roman Britain and the English Settlements* (1937), 85

22. Suetonius, *Galba*, 7

23. Suetonius, *Claudius*, 17

24. Suetonius, *Vespasian*, 4

25. Dio Cassius, lx, 21; Suetonius, *Galba*, 17 and 21; Josephus, *Bell. Jud.*, iii, 4

26. M. P. Charlesworth in *Cambridge Ancient History*, x, 699

27. '*Triumphavitque maximo apparatu*', Suetonius, *Claudius*, 17

28. *C.I.L.*, iii, x, 6809 (=Dessau, *I.L.S.*, 2696)

29. Riese, *Anthologia Latina*, i, pp. 419–26

30. For a full discussion see D. R. Dudley, 'The Celebration of Claudius' British Victories', *Birmingham Historical Journal*, 7. Pt. 1 (1959), 1–17

31. F. Castagnoli, *Bulletin della Commissione Archaeologica del Governatoro di Roma*, 70 (1942), 74

CHAPTER 4

1. Tacitus, *Agricola*, 14

2. Suetonius, *Vespasian*, 4

3. There remains the possibility that the Romans may have been mistaken in identifying two sections of the Durotriges as two separate tribes. It has been suggested by Mr C. E. Stevens that there were two distinct administrative centres of the *civitas*, one at Dorchester and the other at Ilchester (*Proc. Somerset Arch. and*

N.H. Soc., 96 (1951), 188–92) which have been the successors of the two great hill-forts of Maiden Castle (the Dunium of Ptolemy) and Ham Hill

4. Dorothy M. Liddell, 'Report on the Excavations at Hembury Fort', *Proc. Devon Arch. Expl. Soc.,* 2 (1935), 135–75

5. Reverend H. G. Tomkins, *Worlebury, An Ancient Stronghold in the County of Somerset,* 1866

6. *Arch.,* 14 (1803), 90–3. The collection is now in the British Museum

7. D. F. Allen, 'The Origins of Coinage in Britain: A Reappraisal', *Problems of the Iron Age in Southern Britain,* 97–308

8. Professor C. F. C. Hawkes, in *Bagendon* (1961), 46 ff

9. R. E. M. Wheeler, *Maiden Castle, Dorset* (1943)

10. Published like *Maiden Castle* as a Research Report of the Society of Antiquaries, London

11. *Problems of the Iron Age in Southern Britain,* edited by S. S. Frere, 88–90

12. J. Brailsford, 'Early Iron Age "C" in Wessex', *Proc. Prehist. Soc.,* 24 (1958), 101–19

13. This is an over brief summary of Mr D. F. Allen's conclusions in 'The Origins of Coinage in Britain: A Reappraisal', *Problems of the Iron Age in Southern Britain.* His Gallo-Belgic 'C' coinage was introduced into Britain from the south coast and copies of this, his British 'A' and 'B' became the progenitors of the Durotrigian types

14. These two small silver coins, Mack 371 and 372, found near Portsmouth and at Hod Hill respectively, are quite unlike any Durotrigian types and are closer in style to the Catuvellaunian issues. It has even been suggested that they may have stood for *Cogidubnus Rex Atrebatorum et Britannorum* (A. L. F. Rivet, *Town and Country in Roman Britain* (1958), 159), but this is rather fanciful and it is unlikely that Cogidubnus would have been allowed to mint his own coins after A.D. 43

15. Mr D. F. Allen's map in the Introduction to the O.S. *Map of the Iron Age of Southern Britain* (1962)

16. Tacitus, *Annals,* ii, 20

17. *J.R.S.,* 47 (1957), 222

18. The original report was given in the *Proc. Soc. Ant.,* 4 (1856–9), but a reappraisal by Colin A. Gresham appeared in *Arch. J.,* 96 (1939), 114–31

19. Kathleen M. Kenyon, 'Excavations at Sutton Walls, Hereford-shire, 1948–1951', *Arch. J.*, 110 (1953), 66–83. The evidence of decapitation here suggests that some of these victims had been executed

20. *V.C.H., Somerset*, I, p. 295; *Proc. Somerset Arch. and N.H. Soc.*, 53 (1907), 181; 60 (1923), 49–53; 70 (1924), 104; 72 (1926), etc.

21. J. A. Steers, *The Coastline of England and Wales* (1946)

22. I. D. Margary, *Roman Sussex* (1951), Pl. 10. This 'Jockey cap' type of helmet was being replaced about this time by a different type with better neck protection. Helmets similar to that at Lewes are a sure sign of Claudian military activity

23. Now in the Ashmolean Museum, Oxford; formerly in the Medhurst Collection, *Gents. Mag.* (July, 1886); illustrated by E. T. Leeds in *Celtic Ornament* (1933), Fig. 30b

24. Barry Cunliffe, 'Excavations at Fishbourne 1962', *Ant. J.*, 43 (1963), 1–14

25. *Proc. Dorset Arch. and N.H. Soc.*, 52 (1930), 96; 56 (1934), 11

26. *Antiquities of Roman Britain*, 1951, Fig. 21, III, a, 2

27. *Proc. Devon Arch. Expl. Soc.*, 2 (1935), 200; 3 (1938), 67; 4 (1949) 20

28. *Hod Hill*, i, *Antiquities from Hod Hill in the Durden Collection*, J. W. Brailsford, 1962

29. Brief summaries have appeared annually in the *Journal of Roman Studies* (1950–57)

30. Graham Webster, 'The Discovery of a Roman Fort at Waddon Hill, Stoke Abbott, 1959', *Proc. Dorset Arch. and N.H. Soc.*, 82 (1961), 88–108

31. J. B. Calkin, 'An Early Romano-British Kiln at Corfe Mullen, Dorset', *Ant. J.*, 15 (1935), 42–55

32. These latter may have been regarded as lucky charms

33. The outstanding feature of the equipment from Ham Hill is the fine quality of the metalwork. The belt-plates and apron-mounts are probably legionary and so, it would appear, is much of the other equipment which is comparable only to similar items from known legionary fortresses (Listed in *Arch. J.*, 115 (1958), 80–3)

34. Graham Webster, 'An Excavation at Nunnington Park near Wiveliscombe, Somerset', *Proc. Somerset Arch. and N.H. Soc.*, 103 (1959), 81–91

35. Lady Aileen Fox, *Roman Exeter* (1956). Little work has yet been done on the higher part of the town where one might expect the site of a fort

36. *Proc. Dorset Arch. and N.H. Soc.*, 2 (1878), 109

37. The evidence advanced for military ditches at Camerton is insufficient, W. J. Wedlake, *Excavations at Camerton* (1958), 45

38. There is in the British Museum a legionary belt-plate said to have been found at Greenhill, Weymouth

39. The older idea that these burials were the result of a great battle of A.D. 845 between Saxons and Danes (A. Major, *Early Wars of Wessex*, 122) has been totally disproved. The excavator, Mr Philip Rahtz, has suggested that the Roman settlement nearby may have been the missing Iscalis of Ptolemy (O.S. *Map of Roman Britain*, Fig. 1)

40. *J.R.S.*, 14 (1924), 232; *Trans. Bristol and Glos Arch. Soc.*, 61 (1939), 202; 65 (1944), 195; 66 (1945), 294; 68 (1949), 184; 71 (1954), 70; *Arch. J.*, 105 (1960), 89

41. *Roman Colchester*, 1958, Pl. 1

42. The Thracian units in Britain at this stage present a problem. During the reign of Tiberius in A.D. 26, there had been serious trouble in Thrace when the soldiers heard reports that their units were to be broken up, mixed with those of other peoples and sent to distant provinces (*Annals*, iv, 46). Thrace itself was not made a province of the Empire until A.D. 46 but some arrangement must have been made earlier than this with one of the client kings for units to serve in the *auxilia* wherever they were needed

43. *V.C.H., Roman Essex* (1963), 3

44. At Valkenburg, excavated by Professor Van Giffen, *J.R.S.*, 42 (1952), 129 and Pl. xv

45. D. F. Allen, *The Coins of the Coritani* (1963)

46. This is not the generally accepted view which originates from Kathleen M. Kenyon, *Excavations at the Jewry Wall Site, Leicester* (1948), and is followed by A. L. F. Rivet in designating Leicester as a Belgic settlement on the *Iron Age Map of Southern Britain* (1962), and by D. F. Allen, fn. 1

47. Professor S. Frere, *Ant. J.*, 37 (1957), 4

48. *V.C.H., Herts*, IV, 158 and Pl. 1. This helmet, which lacks its cheek-pieces, is now in Colchester Museum. There are actually three punched inscriptions done by three different owners, one of them beginning PP which stands for *primipilaris*, the chief

centurion who commanded the first cohort, the crack unit in the legion

49. This fort was discovered from the air by O. G. S. Crawford as long ago as 1930 (*Antiquity*, 4 (1930), 274; 13 (1939), 455), but still remains to be investigated

50. R.C.H.M., *City of Cambridge* (1959), p. xxxvi

51. Tacitus, *Annals*, xii, 31. Accepting the brilliant textual emendation by Bradley *cunctaque cis Trisantonam et Sabrinam fluvios cohibere parat*

52. T. Davies Pryce, *Ant. J.*, 18 (1938), 29–48

53. The names of these Roman roads are of course of Saxon origin and thus have no association with their original purposes

54. *Arch. J.*, 117 (1960), 40–70. Short popular summaries of the excavations have been published from time to time by the Lincoln Research Committee

55. *J.R.S.*, 39 (1949), 57–78; 46 (1956), 22–36; it is only fair to indicate that Mr Dennis Petch who has carried out further work on these and the *colonia* defences is of the opinion that the timber towers were inserted during the later *colonia* phase

56. *Arch.*, 58 (1903), 573 and Pl. lv; this piece is now in Newark Museum

57. By Mr J. Wacher, report forthcoming

58. By Dr Felix Oswald who worked almost single-handed on this site for many years. Several accounts of this work have been published by the University of Nottingham and in *J.R.S.*, 12 (1922), 249; 13 (1923), 114; 14 (1924), 255; 16 (1926), 36; 17 (1927), 195; 18 (1928), 199; 19 (1929), 193; 22 (1932), 206; 23 (1933), 196; 25 (1935), 77 and 210

59. R. G. Collingwood, *Archaeology of Roman Britain*, 1930, 27

60. *Itinerarium Curiosum*, ii, 1776, 96; this observation which may have been prompted by Horsley, misplaced the Roman town on this side of the river, *Britannia Romana*, 1732, 434

61. Some of these are now in the Margidunum collection in Nottingham University and others in the Castle Museum, Nottingham. A fine military mess-tin also came from this site, *Ant. J.*, 19 (1939), Pl. 87

62. One excavator has already claimed the discovery of a military ditch but its dimensions, eighteen feet wide and three feet deep, leave one in doubt; *J.R.S.*, 47 (1957), 210

63. The result of this work has been published by Nottingham University in three reports, *The Roman Town and Villa at Great Casterton, Rutland* (1951, 1954, 1961)

64. Dr St Joseph had flown over this site in eight of the previous twelve years and nothing had been visible, then the drought of 1959 suddenly revealed the crop-marks of the fort, published in *Great Casterton III*, Pl. ii

65. It would be an achievement to be able to associate this strengthening of the defences with the Boudiccan revolt of A.D. 60, but the pottery evidence is not good enough to make this more than an interesting speculation

66. Stamped 'MATVRVS', the maker, and now in Warwick Museum. It is very similar to others from Gloucester and Broxstowe

67. In Northampton and Kettering Museums respectively, there are also brooches of Hod Hill type from the latter

68. *Ant. J.*, 12 (1932), Pl. xviii, No. 8

69. *Trans. Birmingham Arch. Soc.*, 66 for 1945 and 46 (1950), Pl. xii, Fig. 1, No. 53

70. *Trans. Birmingham Arch. Soc.*, 74 for 1956 (1958), 36

71. *Reliquiae Britannicae Romanae*, ii

72. *Arch. J.*, 115 (1958), Pl. ix B

73. By Charles Green, *J.R.S.*, 32 (1942), 40 and later by Professor Richmond, see next footnote

74. The latest discussion is by Professor I. A. Richmond, *Trans. Bristol and Glos Arch. Soc.*, 81 (1962), 14–16

75. Helen O'Neil, *Trans. Bristol and Glos Arch. Soc.*, 81 (1962), 10–40

76. His name was Dannicus of the Raucae, a tribe in Switzerland

77. Sextus Valerius Genialis, born in Frisia, now part of the Netherlands

78. It is unfortunate that this stone has become separated from its fellows and is now in Gloucester Museum

79. Most of these have been published, *Arch. J.*, 115 (1958), Fig. 3, 71 and Pl. xi B

80. *Ant. J.*, 42 (1962), 3

81. There is part of a Flavian building inscription and one of the men who died there is a soldier of the IInd *Adiutrix*, which was in Britain from only A.D. 71 to 86

82. Dio, lxi, 30

83. Suetonius, *Claudius*, 24

84. Part of one of the large wheels used in lifting the water out of one of the Spanish mines can be seen in the Greek and Roman Life Gallery at the British Museum

85. Silver was extracted from galena, an ore which is mostly lead compounds, the lead pigs are thus the waste products although the metal was widely used. This particular pig was found near Wookey Hole at Charterhouse as long ago as about 1540 and although lost, its inscription was recorded

CHAPTER 5

1. Tacitus, *Annals*, xii, 31–40

2. E. M. Clifford, *Bagendon, A Belgic Oppidum* (1961), 155

3. J. E. Lloyd, *Owen Glendower* (1931), 93–5

4. It must be emphasised that the chronology of the events to be described is tentative. Tacitus provides two fixed points; the arrival of Ostorius Scapula in the autumn of A.D. 47 and the surrender of Caratacus '*nono post anno quam bellum in Britannia coeptum*', i.e. in A.D. 51. The sequence of events is certain, the problem is to try to determine which campaigns were undertaken in each summer. The dating we put forward seems to us reasonable, but we do not claim that it is certain

5. *Trans. Birmingham Arch. Soc.*, 58 for 1934 (1937), 68–83; 72 for 1954 (1956), 1–4

6. *William Salt Arch. Soc.*, for 1927 (1929), 185; *J.R.S.*, 19 (1929), 194

7. This was first noted by Dr St Joseph and considered to be a marching camp, *J.R.S.*, 48 (1958), 95

8. *N. Staffs Field Club* (1912), 139

9. *Trans. Birmingham Arch. Soc.*, 74 for 1956 (1958), 12–25. This bath-house is now under Ministry of Public Building and Works guardianship

10. *J.R.S.*, 43 (1953), 83

11. *Trans. Birmingham Arch. Soc.*, 75 for 1957 (1959), 24–9; and report forthcoming

12. *Trans. Birmingham Arch. Soc.*, 79 for 1960–61 (1964), 11–23

13. *Trans. Birmingham Arch. Soc.*, 69 for 1951 (1953), 50–6

14. *Trans. Birmingham Arch. Soc.*, 73 for 1955 (1956), 100–8

15. D. R. Dudley and Graham Webster, *The Rebellion of Boudicca* (1962), 109

16. All these are in the Rowley House Museum, Shrewsbury; for full details see *V.C.H., Shrops*, I, 244–6

17. *Trans. Birmingham Arch. Soc.*, 69 for 1951 (1953), 54 and Fig. 2; *J.R.S.*, 43 (1953), 84; 48 (1958), 95 and Pl. xiii; a rather better photograph by Mr Arnold Baker has been published in *The Rebellion of Boudicca*, Pl. xii

18. *J.R.S.*, 45 (1955), 88 and Pl. xix

19. In the interim reports in *Ant. J.*, 1956–62

20. The characteristics of the three phases now established are: 1. trenches filled with clean sand showing buildings erected on sterile ground; 2. trenches filled with sand but also with pieces of clay and charcoal showing that timber buildings with clay walls had been built; and 3. wide trenches where the final phase building had been grubbed out by the demolition parties. The evidence from the baths has been confirmed by a section through the Roman street north of this building. Three periods of timber buildings have been found to underlie the first street, showing that the timber phases definitely preceded the setting out of the street plan

21. *Trans. Birmingham Arch. Soc.*, 42 for 1938 (1943), 27–31

22. *Trans. Worcs Arch. Soc.*, 39 for 1962 (1963), 55–8

23. Summarised by Mr George Boon in *Monmouth Antiquary*, 1.2 (1962), 28–33

24. V. E. Nash-Williams, *The Roman Frontier in Wales* (1954), 4, considered it, merely on size, to be a marching camp. Recent work by Dr M. Jarrett has produced a hint of pre-Falvian occupation

25. Tacitus, *Annals*, xiv, 31

26. J. K. S. St Joseph, 'Aerial Reconnaissance in Wales', *Antiquity*, 35 (1961), 269

27. Cf. Tacitus, *Agricola*, 25, where Agricola learns from Caledonian prisoners of the alarm caused by the appearance of the Roman Fleet off the coast of Scotland

28. This work has been carried out by the Devon Archaeological Exploration Society under Lady Fox and Dr Ravenhill and we are grateful for this information in advance of publication

29. Tacitus, *Annals*, xii, 33, '*sed tum astu locorum fraude prior, vi militum inferior . . .*'

30. *Antiquity*, 35 (1961), 270

31. Tacitus, *Annals*, xii, 34–5

32. Tacitus, *Histories*, iv, 23; v, 16

33. Tacitus, *Agricola*, 37; *Annals*, xiv, 37

34. Tacitus, *Histories*, iv, 71

35. Tacitus, *Annals*, xiv, 36–8, describes the review, the speech of Caratacus, and the special session of the Senate

36. Zonaras, ii, 7

37. Syphax, Livy, xxx, 13; Perseus, Livy, xlv, 7–8; Plutarch, *Aemilius Paullus*, 26

CHAPTER 6

1. *Annals*, xii, 39–40

2. Trial excavations were conducted at this site in 1964 by Dr Michael Jarrett, to whom we are indebted for this information, and for allowing us to see the manuscript of an unpublished article on early Roman campaigns in Wales

3. Large temporary camps are known at Blaen Cwm Bach and Twyn-y-Briddallt (Glamorganshire), but these hardly qualify for the Tacitean word *praesidia*. The possibility of early forts at Hereford and Abergavenny should not be forgotten

4. Tacitus, *Annals*, iv, 23

5. '. . . *ut quondam Sugambri excisi aut in Gallias traiecti forent, ita Silurum nomen penitus extinguendum.*' *Annals*, xii, 39

6. '. . . *ac praecipua Silurum pervicacia, quos accendebat vulgata imperatoris vox. . . .*' *id. ib.*

7. E.g. in geology, Silurian limestone; in literature, the Silurist poets, etc.

8. Quintilian, *Institutio Oratoria*, vi, 3, 68

9. On Manlius Valens see Dio, lxvii, 14, 5

10. '... *et auxerat potentiam, postquam capto per dolum rege Carataco instruxisse triumphum Claudii Caesaris videbatur.*' Tacitus, *Histories* iii, 45

11. '... *sed post captum Caratacum praecipuus scientia rei militaris Venutius.* ...' Tacitus, *Annals*, xii, 40

12. For Stanwick see R. E. M. Wheeler, *The Stanwick Fortifications* (Society of Antiquaries Research Report, xvii), 1954

13. '*valida et lecta armis iuventus regnum eius invadunt . . .*' id. ib.

14. Text and translation of selected passages of *Y Gododdin*, the poem in which this exploit is recorded, may be found in *The Burning Tree* by Gwyn Williams (1956), 22 f

15. His full names were Quintus Petilius Cerealis Caesius Rufus. We owe this information to Mr Anthony Birley

16. '(*Venutius*) *quisuper insitam ferociam et Romani nominis odium propriis in Cartimanduam reginam stimulis accendebatur.*' Tacitus, *Histories*, iii, 45

17. '... *mox Didius Gallus parta a prioribus continuit, paucis admodum castellis in ulteriora promotis, per quae fama aucti officii quaereretur.*' Tacitus, *Agricola*, 14

18. See V.C.H. *City of York*, 322. In 1964 Mr Peter Wenham, excavating near the cathedral, produced from his lowest levels pottery which would fit very well into this context, and may well represent traces of marching camps or early forts below the later legionary fortress

19. For Little Chester see Graham Webster in *Archaeological Journal*, 115 (1958), 63; for Templeborough see John Clarke in *Roman and Native in North Britain*, ed. I. A. Richmond (1958), 36

20. For his epitaph (now in the Museo Romano at Rome) see *C.I.L.*, vi, 13272 and *L'Année Epigraphique*, 1953, nr 253. His significance is discussed by E. R. Birley, *Britain and the Roman Army* (1953), 1–9

21. On this subject see Grace Simpson, *Britons and the Roman Army* (1964)

Index

INDEX

INDEX